INVEST YOUR TIME

WORK LESS, ACHIEVE MORE, MASTER YOUR LIFE

MATT SANDRINI

Written by Matt Sandrini,
published by Time Zillionaire Ltd.

www.timezillionaire.com

© 2019 Matt Sandrini

All rights reserved. No portion of this book may be reproduced in any form without permission from the publisher, except as permitted by U.S. copyright law.

For permissions contact: help@timezillionaire.com

First Edition.

ISBN: 9781789721478

ISBN (ebook): 9781789721485

For information about special discounts available for bulk purchases, sales promotions, fund-raising and educational needs, contact book@timezillionaire.com

If a tree falls in a forest
and no one is around to hear it,
does it make a sound?

To you, the reader.
Thank you for giving me a voice.
Your friend,

Matt Sandrini

TABLE OF CONTENTS

Introduction: Working More, Achieving Less	9
Chapter One: Why We Never Have Time	18
Chapter Two: Procrastination On Tap	32
Chapter Three: How To Free Up Time	46
Chapter Four: Go Beyond The Clock	66
Chapter Five: Life-Changing Daily Actions	77
Chapter Six: The Structure To Be Unstructured	92
Chapter Seven: How To Own Your 24 Hours	107
Chapter Eight: Accomplish More, Faster	125
Chapter Nine: Multiply The Value Of Your Time	143
Chapter Ten: Leverage: Expand Beyond Yourself	158
Chapter Eleven: Back To The Future	171
Chapter Twelve: What Now	186

INTRODUCTION
WORKING MORE, ACHIEVING LESS

"It is not death that a man should fear, but he should fear never beginning to live."

Marcus Aurelius

I was stuck in the lobby of the Marriott Hotel.

That might actually sound appealing, but it was 11:37 pm and I wanted to go to bed.

Instead, I was sitting on a barstool crunching numbers into a spreadsheet, my laptop glaring back at me.

Next to me, my manager staring with bloodshot eyes.

Or at least that's how I remember it.

It was my second week on the job and things weren't going the way I imagined them.

That night, I went to bed at 1:00 am tired, frustrated, and deflated.

I spent hours on a useless task that could have been automated. Or completed by a machine. I felt like my time wasn't worth anything.

I didn't like that feeling.

That same week, I started learning everything I could about that damn document.

I didn't know the first thing about spreadsheets. Last time I saw one, it was when my dad showed me how useful it was to put numbers into a document and then…something happened. I wasn't interested.

But this time, I was going to become a master.

First, the technical element. Every day, I would search new formulas and ways to make my daily work more efficient. The more I learned, the more time I freed up to learn new tricks and improve my work. I practised daily.

Then, the human element. I kept track of who was supposed to send me the right information and when, and then created systems to make it easier for them to stick to the deadline. Send them a reminder in advance. Talk to them at the start of the week to prevent blockers.

In a few weeks, it became a well-oiled machine: the document was always ready on time, and I had become the go-to guy to make processes and documents extremely efficient. The project leader commended my efforts from the HQ.

I made things so efficient that my work days were getting shorter. First, I started finishing all my tasks by 3 pm.

Then, that became 1 pm. At the latest.

Everything worked smoothly, and that was the problem.

Because everyone else stayed in the office until past 6 pm, I was expected to do the same.

One day, my manager called me to the side. She wasn't happy.

"You're always the first one to leave the office", she said.

I was back to square one.

I wasn't even assigned more work. So for the next month, I would spend two hours on my tasks and…the final three or four colouring cells and changing the formatting ten times. It was boring as hell (though I have never seen such beautiful spreadsheets).

I was being punished for being efficient and doing great work.

My tasks were done by lunchtime, everyone was more than happy about the results, and yet… that didn't matter. I had to stay in and wait for the imaginary bell to ring.

Once again, I felt that my time wasn't worth anything.

It didn't help that I was spending 4 nights every week in a hotel, in the middle of nowhere. Away from home, away from friends, away from my girlfriend. Every Monday at 4am, I trudged to the train station to do it all again.

With less than 3 days per week at home, my personal time was spread thin between important people and life admin. I felt like I was never able to look for a different position or learn a new skill.

I was stuck.

I needed a different strategy. I didn't want for things to become more efficient, I wanted them to be effective. To do that, I needed to regain control over my schedule and my location. I decided to go to my manager and negotiate one extra workday from home per week. I had demonstrated my worth: they trusted me, and they needed my quality work.

I remember rehearsing on my train to the office: "How can I make it easy for my manager to agree?" I needed to phrase my request from her point of view.

"I have an idea. I want to work from home on Fridays AND Mondays. Not having to travel will save me a ton of time, and everyone will get the main document two hours in advance."

She said yes. Beautiful.

Here's what happened next. On my three days in the office, I would prep all the work to be done on my Friday and Monday from home. I had broken down the process into two daily milestones, so I could know whether I was behind on the plan.

Every Thursday by 3pm, I completed all my work due up to the next Tuesday.

All I had to do was work one hour on Friday (when I received the last update) and then drip feed the work back to my manager when she expected it.

Finally, I had freed up precious time. Instead of having to colour spreadsheets and stay in the same seat for hours, I had freedom. For four days a week.

In the beginning, I just used that freedom to browse the internet, do my laundry, go to the post office, read a book. I wasn't very intentional with it. But very quickly, I started to invest my time.

I started learning new skills. I didn't want to colour spreadsheets for much longer, and I knew I had generated a golden opportunity for me to create something else and make the most of my time.

I practised technical drawing, studied product design processes, and become obsessed with crowdfunding campaigns. People were creating products from ideas, and then raising money before having to manufacture a single unit. I was fascinated.

It didn't take long for me to invest my extra time and new skills into a business.

One day I walked to the office toilet and called a friend of mine. By the end of the call, we decided that we were going to launch a product. We committed.

At this point, I hit another cap: it was difficult to manage life and a full-time job while running a business. I had to step up my game one more time.

I was still away for half of the week, which meant that the remaining time was very "precious" for my social life, my relationship with my girlfriend, and even taking care of life admin. I had to find ways to compress even more into my weekdays.

I started optimising every single task I was involved in even more. Then, I started booking meetings with myself. I wanted to leverage time alone to reduce distractions, but also to work on "extracurricular" activities whenever I was done.

As a consequence of my absolute focus, the quality of my work improved, and once again my team was commended for the weekly documents arriving before the deadline and continuing to improve. I was assigned more responsibility, and that felt good. Bring it on.

After a few months, I was ready to transition fully onto the business I was starting (or so I thought).

It was time to speak to my manager, and I was terrified: I expected her to be really angry at me. Instead, she gave me a warm smile of approval: she knew that's what I really wanted.

In my first business, I got stuck once again. Time was all I had, and I was throwing it all away. Following the myth of the "hustle," I spread myself thin across anything I could be doing. Being great at optimising tasks became a curse: now I could fit more useless things in my day and stay busy without seeing any tangible results. My day was all over the place. I kept waking up tired and unmotivated, and I had zero clarity. I was putting in so many hours only to see limited results: that's when I started questioning the value of time once again.

In a few months I was bankrupt in every area of life but money: my friendships had shrunk, my relationship was withering, my mental health was faltering, and I was skinny and underweight. Again, I was in for another tough lesson, as you'll see in the next chapters.

Eventually I learned the real value of time, and in the following pages you will too.

This book was ideated in Bulgaria, started in Greece, and finished in London. I spent 6 months living in 6 different countries, all while growing my business, expanding my remote team, launching a new product, and even publishing a book. This book.

I coach top entrepreneurs to grow faster, I'm surrounded by inspiring friends, and I can visit my mum abroad for as long as I want.

I am in the best shape of my life, I can speak multiple languages, and last year I learned how to sketchnote and use digital watercolour.

Work sustains my life, and my life sustains work. Because, as you'll see in chapter four, there is no such thing as work-life balance.

I'm not saying this to brag: life will always be a work in progress. I know mine is.

I am just an example of how you can expand the value of your own time by making your own decisions. Time is all we have: when we run out of it, everything else is worthless.

It's also the only non-renewable resource, as you'll see in chapter seven. Yet, we tend to take time for granted, waiting for a magical moment when everything will work in our favour, the planets will align, and everyone else will give us permission to live on our own terms.

In the meantime, the sands keep flowing.

In this book, you will learn timeless principles you can apply to grow your business faster, create a lifestyle you love, and impact others, all while working less and focusing on the right things.

When you master the game of investing your time, any change is possible.

I'm excited to share this journey with you.

Let's get started.

CHAPTER ONE
WHY WE NEVER HAVE TIME

> *"Time is a created thing.*
> *To say 'I don't have time,' is like saying,*
> *'I don't want to."*
>
> Lao Tsu

It was early January, and I was sitting in a cold coworking space. On a Sunday.

We were the only two people in the whole building, and for some reason, the heating wasn't working.

I was too excited to notice my breath in the cold: that day, I was going to buy a domain and start a blog.

Earlier that week, I read a stat that stuck with me.

Worldwide, the average life expectancy is 70.5 years.

That's over 37 million minutes.

"We're all born millionaires", I realised.

And yet, not every minute is the same.

Would you rather live 40 million miserable minutes, or 40 million minutes of passion, growth, and fulfilment?

Measuring the quantity of time isn't good enough. In fact, it's almost irrelevant: it's the quality and impact of that time that makes you time rich.

How to value time

Time is a weird concept. You can't accumulate it, you can't pass it on, buy it, or exchange it, and it goes at a constant pace of one minute per minute.

They say "time is money", but you cannot really quantify its value.

Let's pick how you **spend money** over a set period of time: it's never constant.

Imagine going to a restaurant. You stay for a couple of hours, and pay for a (hopefully great) experience. Let's say you paid $100. Does that mean your time is worth $50/hour?

What if you eat at McDonald's the next day?

How you spend money isn't a reliable way to quantify the value of your time.

So let's take how you **get paid** instead: again, it's not constant.

If everyone has 24 hours, why do some people get paid $7.25 per hour, and others $10,000 for a single phone call?

In most jobs, you only get paid for the amount of hours you dedicate to work: does that make your day's other 16 hours worthless?

Neither spending nor earning money seems to be a reliable way to quantify the value of time.

Here's the truth: time isn't worth anything per se.

It's the value you create with that time, for yourself and for others, that makes it either precious or worthless.

Let me repeat the bad news for you, in case you missed it.

First, time has no intrinsic value. Your time is worthless.

It's what you do with it that generates value, for yourself and for others.

Second, you have no control over how fast time flows (and it's going fast).

That leaves you with only one variable to influence: the **value** of that time.

This book will show you how.

The myth of time management

I tried really hard not to yawn. In school, my history professor could talk for...ages, and never get to the point. No one ever listened, and he was so immersed in his own blabber, that he didn't even notice people falling asleep halfway through the lecture.

It always felt like he could slow down time: seconds became as long as minutes, and every hour felt like five or more.

Today, every time I have a conversation with someone saying "I need excellent time management" or "I cannot manage time," I wish I could send them back to one of those lectures and experience how to slow down time.

People that want to manage time play a losing game: time will always move at the same speed of one minute per minute. You can try to work harder and stretch the day out into the night, looking for that 25th hour that will give you an edge over everyone else...only to find out you cannot manage time. 24 hours is all you get—it's a fair game.

The only variable you can manage is how you move through time: that is, the choices that you make every day while the clock is ticking.

Your daily choices will determine whether you are spending time or investing it.

Spending time keeps you stuck in a constant loop of instant gratification, never increasing the quality and the value of your time.

Investing time, on the other hand, keeps expanding the value of your time, in the present and in the future.

Confused? Let me explain.

Spending time

You wake up feeling groggy: you had awful sleep last night.

You snooze that alarm clock four times, and finally roll to your side and get out of bed.

Slowly, you make your way to the kitchen, only to find out you've run out of milk. After getting ready, you finally make your way to the office: time to get to work. You hate the commute, but are looking forward to working with your team.

Let's take a close look at that quick snapshot: what do you notice?

None of those conditions were created in the present.

Your energy levels weren't made today: they depend on what you had for dinner, where you went to sleep, whether you relaxed (or got wired!) before bed. It was created in the past.

Where you woke up, that also is the result of the past: like you buying a bed, or renting a flat. Same with whatever's in the fridge. Today's breakfast was decided during yesterday's shopping.

Your work? That didn't start today either. And even if it's your first day, that opportunity was created days, weeks, even months ago.

The friendships you have today, the skills you count on, even this very book you are reading (and likely bought a few days ago): all options that were chosen in the past.

Your present reality was created in the past.

You have very little impact over changing your present.

Change in life happens like a cruise ship turning: it takes time, and it keeps moving forward while it's changing course. There is a lag between the decision to adjust the rudder, the action, and the final change in direction.

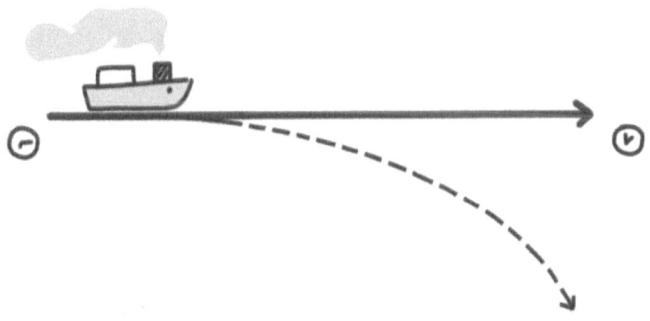

The moment you decide to start a business will decide your future moves.

The moment you buy food at the supermarket will determine your future meals.

The moment you book a great holiday will shape a future experience.

There is always a lag between a decision and its manifestation.

That leaves you with very little influence over your present. All you can do is make decisions that will determine the choices available to your future self.

Just like the set of choices and events you face today were determined in the past.

We tend to ignore this rule, and constantly look for present gratification and immediate results: quick entertainment to avoid boredom, a comfortable solution to today's problem, overspending on credit, settling for friends that are "good enough."

This keeps you stuck in a loop that generates zero value for your future self.

Best case scenario, tomorrow you will wake up in the same situation, facing the same problems (just like a scene from the movie "Groundhog Day"). By constantly looking for small, immediate results, each day is separate from every other: you can never look back and benefit from yesterday's actions until you start focusing on making tomorrow better. Instead of benefitting from a lifetime of work, you are limiting yourself to 24 hours.

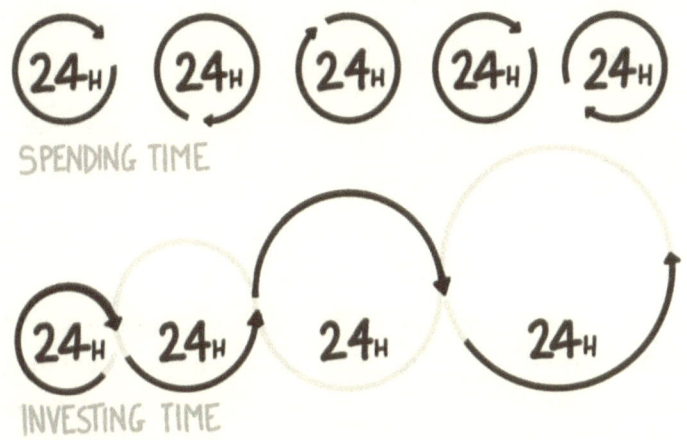

It's a selfish attitude: so selfish that you can't even help yourself.

If you feel stuck in your job, staying comfortable and not looking for alternatives is selfish and short-sighted.

If you want to meet new amazing friends, spending the afternoon playing video games is selfish.

If you envy other people's ability to learn skills, choosing gossiping over learning is selfish: it's all about your present self rather than your future self.

Spending time makes you feel stuck: the same people, the same problems, the same opportunities, the same information (and lack thereof).

Notice how the difference isn't really about the activities you choose, but the intention behind them. Spending time looks for a quick fix over real lasting change, seeks immediate comfort over growth, and has very limited positive impact on the future. Everything is selfishly about today.

This lack of intentionality is expanded to its extreme in "wasting time."

Remember, time goes at the same speed, so you can't literally throw it in the bin. The only thing you can do is focus on things and activities you have no interest in: as long as you're being intentional and doing something that you actually want to do, there is no way to waste time. For example, watching Netflix isn't a waste of time unless you really wanted to do something else. On the other hand, spending time with your spouse while your mind really is at the office, is a total waste of time.

Wasting time doesn't depend on the activity, but on your intention.

> *"Time you enjoy wasting is not wasted time."*
>
> *Marthe Troly-Curtin*

Investing time

Investing time, on the other hand, chooses activities that have a positive impact that go beyond the present moment and into the future.

Investing time does not mean leading a boring life of self-sacrifice waiting for a future pay off. It doesn't mean being busy all the time, spending countless hours at the office, or sacrificing your present hoping for a future gain. That is selfish too, as it takes tomorrow for granted, and focuses on a present feeling of immediate validation.

Investing time focuses on activities that have an impact in the present and beyond it.

Examples are creating a fun memory, facing a life-changing challenge, doing an intense workout, sharing an experience with a great friend, learning a new skill…anything that will have a positive effect beyond the present time of that experience.

When I went bungee jumping with a friend, the whole experience took around four hours. I was terrified and excited at the same time: I was scared of heights, and the idea of being flung up and down in the air terrified me. Floating in mid-air at zero gravity was an amazing experience that is still with me to this day. In fact, it created a lifelong memory, helped me get past my fear of heights, and grew our friendship closer.

I couldn't have invested that time better.

Choosing a job that you are passionate about will make you grow and contribute to others.

Creating memories with special people will make your relationships grow and support others.

Learning a new skill will grow your abilities and create new opportunities for yourself and others.

Taking an afternoon off to watch a silly TV show and recharge will also support your growth and enable you to give others your best time.

Notice how once again, the difference isn't really about the activities you choose, but the intention behind them. Investing time looks at the bigger picture, creating growth and impact beyond yourself and beyond your present moment. Everything fits into a bigger puzzle.

Investing time makes you experience growth: deeper relationships, new problems and bigger opportunities, new skills and new abilities.

Whereas the benefits of spending time are short-lived, investing time creates ripple effects that stack up and compound: great connections will support your career, which will support your well being, which will facilitate positive choices…and so on.

Reading 365 books a year without taking any action would still be spending time.

Reading one life-changing book and transforming your attitude, that's investing time.

Coming up with your nth business idea instead of looking for a sale is spending time.

Finding your first small client and learning to get past your fear is investing time.

Going to the gym only to check your phone while slouching on the treadmill is spending time.

Doing a 20-minute super intense workout every week that pushes your limits is investing time.

See the difference? **Intention.**

Spending time is draining, because you have to start from scratch every day, and your actions are in competition.

Investing time is energising, because you see real progress, can line up your actions like dominos, and you can stack up your past wins.

Investing your time can be as simple as using 5 minutes a day to learn a new skill, relaxing by cooking a meal, or exploring a new part of town with a great friend.

The compass is not short-term drudgery, but long-term passion: investing your time is only possible when you choose a clear direction for your story. It's totally ok to adjust along the way, but when you're only concerned with the day-to-day, you won't have the perspective to be intentional with your choices.

What now

To get some perspective, do this quick exercise.

First, think back 3-5 years. How different was your life then? How different were you?

Take a few minutes to write down what changed, and really think about it.

This will show you how much things can change in just a few years, whether you actively want them to or not.

Now, look forward 3-5 years. What do you want your life to look like then? How different do you want to be?

Take some time to really explore what you want to happen. I recommend taking a sheet of paper or a blank document, and writing a description of "a day in the life of my future self."

Imagine a day in the future, starting from the moment you wake up to the moment you go to bed: it doesn't have to be a special day, just visualise and notice what you see.

Then, make a list of the things that stood out: what do you need to accomplish between now and then?

Finally, let's make that list more actionable and less overwhelming by focusing on what will bring you disproportionate results.
You will find that many of the objectives on the list are but a

natural byproduct of a few others. For example, if your list includes:

- *Building a 6-figure remote business*
- *Visit Bali for a month*
- *Pay off my credit card debt*

Achieving the first goal will help check off the other two. But if you focus on all of them, you will get distracted, focusing on making these objectives happen separately instead of together.

Other goals or images from your 3-5 year vision will feel almost unrealistic for your current level; it's ok to freeze a few and focus on 1-2 big goals that will change your situation and free up more resources (time, capital, health, confidence, connections…) to then move on stronger than ever.

As we'll see in the next chapter, this is the power of aligning your actions, so they compound over time and support each other.

This quick exercise will give you an idea of your future direction, which you can use to set goals, and choose your actions and options with intention. This clarity will come in handy on your path to investing time.

CHAPTER TWO
PROCRASTINATION ON TAP

"You cannot escape the responsibility of tomorrow by evading it today

Abraham Lincoln

How often do you say 'yes' to something, only to regret it moments later?

43% of Americans have been carrying a credit balance for over two years, at an average of over $6,000 at the time of this writing.[1] Things aren't much better on this side of the Atlantic, with 89% of credit card debt staying (once again) for over 2 years in the UK.[2]

---

[1] Michelle Crouch, *Survey: Who is most likely to carry credit card debt?*, 2017
2 Bank of England, *Statistics*, 2019

When you take on debt, you're essentially spending future money.

You can leverage that debt to make more money for your future self (as we'll see in chapter ten), or you can spend it on things that won't generate any income and essentially spend your future self's money.

For example, if you use that debt to buy a holiday or a new handbag you can't afford, you are taking away future resources. It may not be today's problem, but it's still your problem.

Borrowing money isn't free either. Unless you have a 0% fee, you will have to pay it off with interest (while you watch the things you bought on credit lose value every day). The longer you wait, the more you will have to pay back. It's a big F-you to your future self.

Instead of escaping your present by complicating your future, you should invest your time to change your present situation.

The goal is to upgrade your daily lifestyle for good, not a temporary escape from a daily environment you hate.

Anyway, you didn't pick up a book about debt. So what has this got to do with time?

Credit card mindset expands beyond money, and affect the way you manage all your resources, including time.

When I was a kid, I never made my own bed in the morning: I was a rebel.

Making my bed was unnecessary, and was stealing precious time from my "clearly" busy day. By refusing to make my own bed, I was playing by my own rules instead of everyone else's. Plus, it was so unnecessary. Or that's how it felt.

At the end of each day, I was the one going back to a messy bed. I was being a rebel, but only against myself.

On a bad day, that sucked: when I came back home, my day was already a mess, and now my bed was a mess too. It made me feel like I was always on my own. There was nothing to ground me, catch me in a bad moment, and start setting things right.

One day, I realised that every time I wasn't making my own bed, I was giving a big F-you to my future self. The only way to come back to a nice bed was to make it in the morning.

No other way: my morning actions were determining the results I would find in the evening. They were also setting the tone for the whole day: be messy and disregard future consequences, or be mindful and create the best starting point to build a great day on.

It wasn't just about making my bed, it was about creating my future.

Whenever we make an easy decision in the present that will have negative consequences at a later time, we are borrowing from the future.

We won't benefit from any positive consequence: actually, we will have to sort out the mess, eventually.

Not making your bed in the morning means you'll go back to a messy home, tired.

Not doing the washing up means that you'll wake up to a pile of stinky plates encrusted with dried food.

Not going to sleep when it's bed time means you'll start the day feeling tired, groggy, and will get less done (so you'll have to skip sleep again).

Not having that uncomfortable conversation means another day of doubting your own choices.

All these examples have one thing in common: they keep the present easy without realising the hidden costs in the future, which often become greater with time.

They forget that today's present was yesterday's future–it's too late to influence it now, but we can influence our starting point for tomorrow. Short term action is selfish.

In fact, it's so selfish, it hurts your future self.

Planning the next week every Friday is a great way to give your future self a leg up.

Often, when I work with business owners to take them from overwhelmed to high-performers, the objection I get in the beginning is "I don't have time to plan my week."

By now, you should know that is total BS: we all get the same amount of time.

But let's focus on that example for a moment: not planning your next day in the evening may save you 10 minutes right now. Not planning your week, one hour.

Great. Except, tomorrow you'll be all over the place (once again), reacting to any possible action, with no clear direction and scraping the barrel for an extra 5 or 10 minutes.

By saving 10 minutes in the present (and not planning your day or week), you are throwing tomorrow in the bin. Get ready for another deja-vu.

When you invest your time, you take an action in your present which will have positive ripple effects in the future: learning a new skill, fostering a great friendship, creating a memory, planning your actions, and much more.

When you accumulate time debt, on the other hand, your current actions will have negative consequences in your future (often to be paid back with interest): working late into the night (and then sleeping at your laptop the next day), postponing a difficult conversation (and then having to face the consequences), taking your health and fitness for granted, or looking for a quick temporary fix to a challenge you don't want to face.

It's the time equivalent of credit card mindset. Remember: today's choices will determine tomorrow's starting point.

The cost of procrastination

Time debt accumulates through any decision that is easy in the present, and will have a negative impact on the future: this includes avoiding to take action right now, waiting for a "perfect moment" or for things to sort themselves out.

Things never stay the same: when you put off taking action, you are giving more time and resources to the very thing you want to change. You are reinforcing bad behaviours, giving space to negative circumstance, and taking your current opportunities for granted. When you finally decide to take action (if ever), it will be even more difficult to do so.

You'll be left with less time and more consequences to undo.

Not writing that book you have in you reinforces your identity as a non-author and your ability to avoid writing. The longer you wait, the more difficult it will be to finally start.[3]

---

[3] If you're ready to write a book, I recommend contacting Chris at writing-coaching.com to guide you through the whole process.

Not leaving a job you hate teaches you that it's ok to stay stuck without making the most of your gifts. The longer you wait, the more difficult it will be to find something better.

On a micro, everyday level, this manifests in procrastination: constantly delaying taking action. Procrastination is a manifestation of fear: instinctively, we do not like change. In fact, most of the time we'd rather be unhappy than uncertain.

Procrastination is showing you what's important: you are avoiding it, because you know it's what will have a real impact on your life, your business, and your growth.

Procrastination can manifest two ways: **avoidance** and **busyness.**

Avoidance is when you know you should really work on that new product launch but decide to play video games instead. It's when you distract yourself from taking action by doing something completely unrelated.

Avoidance is easy to spot, and a quick fix is to do your meaningful work in a distraction-free environment, away from interrupting people and tempting activities.

Busy procrastination, on the other hand, is much sneakier. It keeps you busy working day and night, creating the perfect plan, starting new tactics, and overcomplicating things.

This keeps you busy and spread thin, so you never have to face what really scares you. The same happens with perfectionism.

Entrepreneurs are particularly vulnerable to busy procrastination, committing to a new tactic only to switch to a more promising "shortcut" once things start to become complex or show some sort of results. Procrastination is a shield against fear of failure.

Procrastination may keep you (temporarily) safe from fear of change and fear of failure, but at what cost?

Every time you avoid growing your business, you choose not to talk to that person that caught your attention, or you decide to put off learning a new skill, is one more time you teach yourself that it's ok to accept a low standard of behaviour and mediocre results. The more you enforce that lesson, the more difficult it will become to change in the future.

In the meantime, opportunities pass you by and you keep running out of time.

Next time you catch yourself procrastinating, picture the cost of ten more years of avoiding taking action: how will you feel then? Use that emotion as fuel to take action.

If you keep opening new opportunities and tasks and never close any, remember that no one ever got a medal for starting something, only for finishing: start fewer things, and become a serial closer.

Procrastination and time debt are on the rise: 20% of the population are chronic procrastinators, and 95% procrastinate. That's four times as many as 40 years ago.[4]

In the age of endless choice and constant information overload, it's increasingly difficult to say no without feeling like you're missing out. However, this takes you away from what really matters to you and from your purpose. In the next chapter, you will learn how to say no and focus on what brings you disproportionate results.

For now, here are some common everyday manifestations of credit card mindset. Spot them, so you can stop them.

Everyday time debt

Remember, your 24 hours aren't worth anything. It's the value you generate with those 24 hours that makes you either time rich or time poor.

Whenever your present actions affect your future resources and baseline negatively, you are accumulating time debt:

---

[4] James Surowiecki, *Later. What does procrastination tell us about ourselves?*, 2010

Business.com Editorial Staff, *5 Tell-Tale Signs You're a Chronic Procrastinator*, 2017 instead of stacking up positive effects for you future, you collect liabilities which you will have to deal with in the future.

In **health and fitness**, not looking after yourself means that your performance will drop across all aspects of life. Exercise is shown to increase productivity by 21% on the same day, lower stress, and increase feel-good hormones like endorphins.[5]

Putting your health on pause is a lie we tell ourselves: as a system, the body is in constant change and adaptation. So if you spend most of your day sitting in a chair, guess what? Your body will adapt to make you world-class at sitting in a chair. In the meantime, your muscles shrink and shorten, your metabolism slows down, and you'll find yourself with a much lower baseline than when you started. You will have to invest lots of future time to get back to where you were (all while your performance is compromised).

In **business** and **career**, waiting for the perfect moment to make your next move means that opportunities will go past you while your skills become obsolete. In the meantime, you are training yourself to stay stuck where you are.

In **relationships**, avoidance will come back to haunt you. When I started my first business, I thought I could "freeze" my friendships while I hustled my way to a product launch. Months later, I found myself with very few friends around me

---

[5] J.C. Coulson, J. McKenna, M. Field, (2008) *"Exercising at work and self-reported work performance"*, International Journal of Workplace Health Management, Vol. 1 Issue: 3, pp.176-197,

(and my romantic relationship in a tough spot). When you are putting off any kind of relationships, you are giving up one of your most important assets. This is a people planet: whether you want to sell a product, create amazing connections, or craft lifelong memories, you cannot achieve anything on your own.

The sleepless cycle

Over 30% of adults in the US suffer from sleep deprivation[6]. This is simply the condition of not getting enough sleep on a regular basis (or sleeping outside your normal rest window).

Sleep deprivation has well researched consequences on your health, metabolism, lifespan, as well as your ability to work (and to accurately gauge your actual productivity).

In fact, studies have shown that moderate sleep deprivation has similar consequences on your ability to work to those of drinking alcohol[7]. After only 17 hours of being active without sleep, your performance level is comparable to that of drinking alcohol past the legal limit for drink driving in the US. This affects reaction time, memory capacity, hand-eye coordination, task speed and execution. After 20 hours or more without sleep, performance levels drop further, but much more steeply: with just 3 more hours, performance levels were comparable to someone having had twice the amount of alcohol: from 0.05% to 0.1% blood alcohol concentration.

---

[6] American Sleep Association, *Sleep and Sleep Disorder Statistics*
[7] Centers for Disease Control and Prevention, *Data and Statistics*, 2012

When you stretch out your day into the evening, trying to add extra hours to your day, all you're doing is borrowing from tomorrow: you will wake up late, feeling tired and more confused.

With a shorter day ahead of you, and your performance drastically reduced, you will not be able to make the most of your day, and will try to stretch your workday out into the evening once again. And so on, so forth.

This is ultimate time debt: by borrowing time from the future, the interest will come back to haunt you in the form of poor productivity and even burnout.

It's ok to have a work sprint if you truly are on a deadline: but when it becomes a lifestyle, it's likely a sign of busy procrastination—you are drinking too much coffee, and not working on the right things.

The sleepless cycle comes from a day not lived fully: either working on tasks that don't get you anywhere, or spending time on activities that do not fulfill you or leave aspects of your life behind. This leaves you with a sense of urgency and disappointment that keeps you up hoping for more. Break the cycle with a good night's sleep (or several) so you can solve the core issue, not the symptom.

Time debt is the worst: it robs your future self of a better start and trades your future opportunities for immediate, fleeting gains. At some point, you will have to deal with the consequences, which can range from a sense of being stuck and directionless, all the way to burnout. In the next chapter, you will learn why being able to say a loud "no" is the antidote to procrastination and time debt.

What now

The first step towards change is awareness. Now that you understand the cost of putting things off (and how you build up your sense of overwhelm), you can change your behaviour to create better opportunities for your future self: adopt an attitude of being your best self.

As you will see in chapter four, life is a system where every part influences every other to create harmony: you cannot put something on "pause" without affecting everything else.

To break out of credit card mindset and avoid time debt, it's key to have a full day, go all in on all the activities that are important to you, and watch them support each other.

In future chapters, you will learn how to quickly plan your day in advance, so you squeeze as much value out of it and make the important fit, all while keeping it fun.

Having a clear direction, as we saw in chapter one, is fundamental to investing your time. Don't forget to download your worksheet to follow along with the book at timezillionaire.com/invest-bonus

In the next chapter, you will learn the one word that can turn you from a procrastinating machine into a high-performer.

CHAPTER THREE
HOW TO FREE UP TIME

"I fear not the man who has practiced 10,000 kicks once, but I fear the man who has practiced one kick 10,000

Bruce Lee

By now you know that your time is limited.

Each of us has 168 hours a week, 52 weeks a year, and about 75 years in our lives on average. We're all running out of runway.

Because of this, there's only so much we can fit into our day, year, and lives. We must choose intentionally. Yet, we seem to develop a default "yes" response to things that have zero impact, and an automatic "no" to what could make a massive difference.

Saying "yes" to another Netflix show is easy, saying "yes" to reading a whole book is difficult.

Saying "yes" to a boring but safe client is easy, committing to launching a product is difficult.

Saying "yes" to the same conversation with the same friends is easy, meeting new inspiring people in your town is difficult.

But which could have disproportionate results?

Yet, most of the time our default position is to say yes to loads of things that don't make any difference. Only to hand out a quick no to the things that could create real impact.

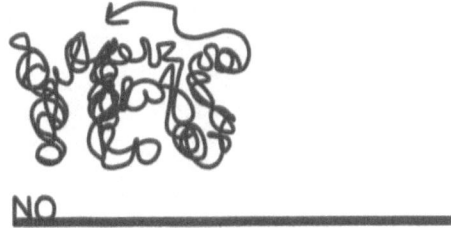

Not only are we hard wired to give our time to the unimportant, we also shy away from the important.

Whenever you say yes, you are actually saying no to everything else you could be doing instead.

Whenever you say no, you are just excluding one possible scenario, and guarding your resources and time for something more purposeful.

Yes closes the door to everything else. No leaves the door open to opportunity.

To be able to say YES to what matters, you have to say no to what doesn't.

When you realise time is the only truly limited resource, you must switch strategies from spreading yourself thin to squeezing as much impact as possible out of every minute.

That's when mastering "no" comes in. You want to override the programming so that you can commit your very limited resources to the right things. By being selective, you can invest your time, and instantly increase the value of your days.

You will create impact, meaningful results, and lifelong memories.

If you find yourself saying "I don't have time to…", you are saying yes to the wrong things (and likely too many things). The instructions in this chapter will help you understand how to create time for what really matters in your life.

But first, to become a master of selection we must understand why we tend to say "yes" so lightly (only to regret it later).

Yes (it's easy)

When you're used to saying yes all the time, it will feel almost impossible to let go. Not only is it your default answer: we are wired to agree to small commitments lightly. Working in the background are several cognitive biases: mental models and shortcuts we subconsciously use to make decisions quickly and efficiently without having to dedicate a ton of time and resources to the most petty conclusion.

To become a master of your time, you must learn to recognise these mental models, so you can use them to your advantage instead of being a victim of them.

Here's what's happening behind the scenes, making you agree to a ton of useless commitments (and keeping you away from what would make a real impact).

Loss aversion (and missed opportunities)

Loss Aversion is the tendency to prefer avoiding losses over acquiring equal gains: in other words, we cling to what we already have more than what we want to have. We would rather not lose $5 than gain $5. Studies have shown that we value resources lost twice as strongly as we do gains. In money terms, it takes a potential win of $10 to risk losing $5.

Saying NO closes a potential opportunity you already had.

It doesn't matter whether it was relevant or impactful, or even if you would have sought out that opportunity in the first place: loss aversion will make it difficult for you to let go and say no. The key is to remember that committing to something means assigning your time to it, and taking it away from any other option.

Letting go of opportunities that are not aligned with your purpose, or just not good enough, is the only way to make space for the important.

Fear of Missing Out

Fear of missing out (or FOMO) is the worry of having made the wrong decisions on how to spend time, and typically manifests in constantly contemplating how things could be different. Whatever you choose, you'll hate your decision.

This brings an inability to commit, and an impatience towards results, always keeping up with other people's (instagram) lifestyle choices.

Decision fatigue

Good decisions have a daily cap. Here's why: many decisions rely on willpower, and our daily willpower is limited. In fact, self-control works like a muscle, weakening with each extra rep until it's too tired to do another one. At that point, our willpower lets go, and we tend to fall back on our default setting or the easiest option.

As we progress through the day, we are more likely to go back to safer decisions, and be subject to a general inability to decide. It's at this point that a light "yes" often sounds like the safest option.

Last time you binge ate in the evening, you probably had just decided you were not going to do it. But yes won.

That's why bad decisions are more frequent in the evening, after a long day at work.

A research study on decision making[8] examined 1,112 parole rulings assigned to 8 judges over a 10-month period. Judges are under a lot of pressure, as they have to hear arguments and take a decision on 14 to 35 parole requests a day with only two breaks in between to rest: a morning snack and a late lunch.

The impact of this relentless schedule is striking: chances of being granted parole peak at 65% at the start of the day and right after each break, and plunge to practically 0% at the end of each shift, the safer decision.

---

[8] Shai Danziger, Jonathan Levav, Liora Avnaim-Pesso, *Extraneous factors in judicial decisions*, PNAS, vol. 108, 17, (2011), pp. 6889 -6892.

Just like in the study, your ability to make decisions, especially good ones, diminishes throughout the day. The more demanding your day is, the more rapidly this decline occurs.

That's why many high-performers are known to always wear the same outfit: Steve Jobs, Mark Zuckerberg, and even former U.S. President Obama are amongst those who intentionally reduce their dressing options to preserve their willpower for bigger choices later in the day.

You don't have to stick to one outfit, but reducing those daily options that have no significant impact on your day will greatly improve your ability to say no.

Here are several things that eat away at your willpower: implementing new behaviours, filtering distractions, making decisions, resisting temptation, suppressing emotion, suppressing impulses, taking tests, trying to impress others, dealing with fear, doing something you don't enjoy, selecting long-term over short-term rewards.

With a plethora of everyday choices, we squander our willpower on things that don't matter, and have none left for really important life decisions.

Psychological distance

Imagine organising your next summer's holiday one year in advance: likely, you will focus on high-level concepts of fun and relaxation. It seems easy.

The closer you get to the holiday though, the more you'll start planning the practical steps: where to stay, what places to visit, how to get to each location, and which restaurants to eat at. In essence, the closer in time you get to an event, the more you will shift your thinking from abstract concepts to more concrete aspects. Sunshine and unicorns will turn into packing and booking.

This phenomenon is called *psychological distance*. Just like events happening in your town seem more actionable and relatable than those happening on a different continent, the same happens through time. **This has consequences on our decision making.**

When planning the future, psychological distance makes commitment blurry and abstract, leading to overcommitment, overlapping tasks, or plans that require more time than what is available.

In a research study, college students were asked to plan their week to accommodate their various activities: when planning for the near future, they took into account how each activity would affect time available on another; when planning the distant future however, they tended to plan as though they had unlimited time and resources. The future is blurry.

Distance through time also makes us underestimate the value of events and outcomes happening in the future, and give more value to immediate events and results.

This also means that an impactful commitment with an outcome in the future (like "learning French") will be discounted, while an immediate small result (such as "watch a film") will gain perceived value from happening closer in time.

Shiny object syndrome

Shiny object syndrome (SOS) isn't as official and medical as it sounds: it's more of a mindset, but its effects can be paralysing. SOS is the inability to stick with a long-term decision, starting things only to leave them as soon as a tactic that seems more promising (or easier) comes along. Shiny object syndrome takes its name from small children getting easily distracted by shiny objects, and wanting to drop everything else in order to chase them.

SOS applies particularly to entrepreneurs: the need to manage risk, and figure out a way towards your goals make business a shiny object minefield.

Instead of sticking to the course and pushing through a difficult patch, sometimes it feels irresistible to switch to a new promising tactic, only to switch again when things get complicated.

Other areas in which SOS manifests regularly are dating, fitness and diets, and any activity that requires consistent action-taking to see any tangible results. SOS is the ultimate yes-trap: you'll be tempted to take a shortcut, only to find out it's actually a detour.

By now, you know how constantly saying "yes" keeps you trapped in a multitude of commitments that don't take you anywhere: saying yes also books up your time and resources, preventing you from choosing better options that will bring disproportionate results to your life, your business, and the important people around you.

We also looked at why you are wired to splurt out an easy "yes", so you can catch yourself next time and change your behaviour through awareness.

Now, let's look at the power of "no" (and why we hate it so much).

No (it's difficult)

You can attempt to learn a hundred martial arts at once: chances are, you'll become mediocre at best. You'll feel like you put in a lot of effort and didn't get anywhere.

You might decide that you want to cultivate 100 friendships: you'll likely feel overwhelmed, and like you're still letting most of them down.

You can choose to start 5 businesses at the same time: you'll probably find yourself with 5x the problems, and ⅕ of the results.

That's because time is the only non-renewable, non-expandable resource we have: you have to choose how to allocate it. Which means you have to choose what doesn't make the cut.

That's why saying yes to everything is a losing strategy: you can't expand time.

So why is "no" so difficult to say?

Peer pressure (people pleasing)

Your peer group is made up of the people in your life that have similar characteristics to yours: from age and gender, to social status, personal interests, and background. The closer they are to you, the more influential they are.

Peer pressure is a compelling need towards wanting to fit in with the group of individuals you identify with in order to be accepted by the group. This derives from our ancestral need to be accepted by the tribe, the only guarantee to our individual survival.

Peer pressure makes it difficult to turn down social commitments, but also to distance yourself from expectations and carve your own path.

This gets even worse for **people pleasers**, who feel a compelling need to please everyone in their social circle by saying yes in the hope of gaining everyone's approval (it never works).

Awareness will help you become more comfortable with saying no. However, you can take this a step further and use peer pressure dynamics to your advantage: by surrounding yourself with like minded individuals aligned to your purpose, peer pressure will support your activities rather than being in competition with them. After all, that's why they say "you're the average of the 5 people you hang out with."

Comfort zone (aversion to change)

We are wired to hate change. Every time an app changes its icon color, I hate it. Only to become terribly fond of it a couple of weeks later.

In one study, a group of participants was shown a painting, and was told it was made in 1905. The second group was shown the same painting, but told it was made in 2005.[9]

The first group found the painting more aesthetically appealing.

Not only do we tend to like things that have been around for a while, brain scans have shown how **we register change like an error**: something is wrong.

Aversion to change keeps you stuck in the comfort zone. Always saying yes to the usual, easy choices that don't take you anywhere, and unable to say no and make space for new

---

[9] Scott Eidelman, Jennifer Pattershall, Christian S. Crandall, Longer is better, *Journal of Experimental Social Psychology*, Vol 46, Issue 6, (2010), pp. 993-998

adventures. When you realise and accept your tendency for comfort and stability, you can slowly train yourself to accept (and even seek) change. Over time, this will bring massive results to your life (and skyrocket the value of your time).

Spreading your bets

Wanting to spread your bets, in business and life, makes you feel safer.

When you are working on many tactics, or launching many products at the same time, it feels that some will *have* to work out (at some point). By meeting many people, it feels like you will find great friendships or an amazing partner. If you read many books, you will inevitably learn new things. Like playing a numbers game, increasing your activity makes you feel like you are increasing your odds of finally getting a result.

SPREADING YOUR BETS

This can lead to taking on too many commitments that you can't really manage, instead of focusing on the few targeted actions that could give you the results that you want. Spreading your bets can sabotage your efforts, and even show a lack of trust that what you are doing will work out. Become a sniper, and say no to anything that will not bring you the results you are looking for.

We are wired to see "no" as a difficult word to say: we don't want to miss out or let other people down, and we hate change. But no makes space for the real, loud yes.

When to say yes

When you say no to the unimportant, you make space for what truly matters.

Imagine if everyone had the same size room: that's your 24 hours. There's only so much you can fit in that room, and if you want to make space for something big and useful (like a bed), you'll have to get rid of all the useless tiny objects lying around.

Now that we've clarified the importance and the power of saying no, it's time to say YES.

Not the easy, reactive yes that clutters your calendar and makes you procrastinate on the important. I'm talking about life-changing, enthusiastic YES.

Quantity vs Quality

Saying yes to new things in quantity gets you exposure to new ideas, new experiences, new challenges, and personal growth. When you are **seeking clarity**, looking for answers, or finding a new strategy to achieve a goal, that's when quantity is your friend.

- *Adding a new channel to find clients or customers?*
- *On the lookout for amazing friends in a new city?*
- *Starting a business (but not sure which one)?*
- *Looking for a great person to date?*
- *Searching for an activity to be passionate about?*

Experimenting with many things by saying yes often will give you quick exposure to options, so you can learn fast what works to give you the results you are looking for.

Once you find it, drop what's not working, whether it's people, activities, goals: say no and move on.

The aim is not to accumulate a ton of commitments, but rather taste different options until you find what you're looking for (or an efficient and fun way to get there).

For example, when I started the Time Zillionaire blog, I had no idea how to drive traffic to my posts and find readers for my content. So for a few months, I tried many tactics to see what could work. Once I found one that produced consistent results (for me, it was writing on Quora), I committed to it and said YES, getting over 2 million views in less than 10 months.

Which brings me to the next point: quality. Once you find what works for you, it's time to **stop trying new things**, and commit with a strong and resounding YES.

Whether it's a diet that boosts your energy, a skill that can change your life, a person that can take you to the next level, or a system that doubles your productivity, commit and drop everything else until it no longer works or you must change things to get to the next level again.

To be able to choose, you need to be clear on what you are looking for. Exposure will help you figure that out, but in the age of infinite choice you need to trust your choice and commit. The imperfect decision made with 100% commitment will bring more impact than the perfect decision with 10% commitment. You have to go all in and make it work.

Once you do that, your life will be filled with meaningful activities, people, and challenges that are aligned with your purpose, not in competition with it. Instead of stuffing life with things you feel lukewarm about, go all in on what makes you passionate: at that point, saying no to everything else will become easy.

What now

Time to implement saying no in your own life, so you can become super-effective.

The first step is to make a list of current projects you have on: include all the regular and recurring activities in your days, from work (or your different business projects) to social activities, learning, and..."wasting" time.

Now look at that list and ask: what's missing? Add a new column to include the important activities you keep postponing.

Then go through the original list, and delete everything that is unnecessary, ineffective, or…just isn't worth your time.

The second step is to look at what actually happens throughout your days, and track how you spend your time for a week or two (even better). Make sure you choose a regular week: if you have any disruptive event (like a conference or a friend visiting), you won't get the insights you are looking for.

You can track how you spend your time using a spreadsheet, a piece of paper, a document, or your calendar. How you do it really doesn't matter. Set a reminder at least twice a day, so you can look back and record how you spent every one-hour increment.

At the end of the two weeks, look back on your activities and add up the time spent on each: you'll likely be stunned at how different it is from what you expected.

Guess what? Time to say no and get rid of ballast: eliminate what shouldn't be there.

To make it easier for you to take action, I have created a free worksheet you can download at

> timezillionaire.com/invest-bonus

Download it now before you forget.

If you're a yes-spray, and find it difficult to turn down commitments you feel "meh" about, here's how to sharpen your "no":

Start to implement a delay to your commitments: instead of saying yes straight away, explain that you need to check your availability and will confirm later. Whether this is two hours or a whole week, it will give you the time (and the psychological distance) to make a rational decision based on the bigger picture.

Write down the cost of saying yes: take a moment to think about the opportunity cost of constantly saying yes. If you're a people pleaser, you might be letting down the people that actually care about you by spreading yourself thin all the time. If you're a procrastinating entrepreneur, you might be sabotaging your business by switching tactics every week. Clarifying the opportunity cost helps defuse that feeling of missing out, and realise you already are (by spreading yourself so thin).

Finally, take your time to clarify what you want and what you are looking for, so you can say a loud and committed YES to what matters most to you.

CHAPTER FOUR
GO BEYOND THE CLOCK

> *"I want to live an exceptional life.
> I'm not seeking balance."*
>
> Grant Cardone

"I juggle too much" is the mantra of the overwhelmed.

When you think of life as a game of juggling, everything is in competition for your limited resources. You see each area as isolated from each other, constantly trying to patch up issues before they get out of control.

The act of juggling means that you take care of one thing at a time while leaving the rest "up in the air". That's until you add too many items to your routine, and can no longer cope with the juggling: once one ball drops, it's game over. In life, that means overwhelm, a sense of being stuck, or even burn out.

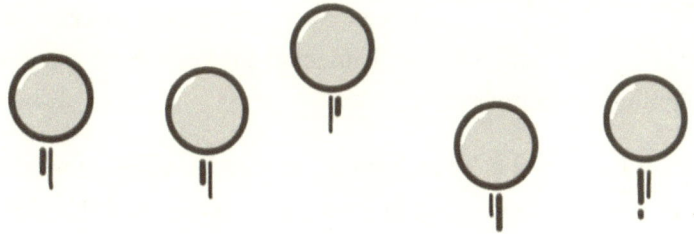

Life (and business) is not made of separate parts: it's a system. Like an ecosystem, each part affects the functioning of the rest.

Working out will make you more productive at work, which will make you more fulfilled, bringing about better social relationships, which will support your personal growth, support positive habits…and so on.

Instead of thinking of juggling separate balls, think of growing a sphere.

The sphere represents the system which is your life: when you focus on growing the sphere, your efforts will be aligned instead of in competition, creating ripple effects across multiple areas.

When I work with entrepreneurs to help them increase their work performance, one of the first things I suggest (i.e. make them do) is to do a micro-workout every morning. With time this will turn into a habit and upgrade to full-on legit workouts.

Most times I suggest this I get incredulous looks: "What's moving my body got to do with business?"

Until, just a few weeks later they all see an increase in happiness, confidence, and mental performance. They're aligning their activities.

Once, I received a letter from a blog reader asking how she could learn a language while taking care of her child. The first thing I asked is how that aligned with her goals and activities, but also whether she could create a fun way to learn while spending time with her baby. She carved out a fun 30-minute window where learning French together became shared quality time–it became a bonding experience.

But we're taught to keep the areas of our lives separate and seek work-life balance.

The thinking behind this is that work should be different from "life," assuming work must be as unpleasant as possible. That's why you need to balance it out with "life."

So the week is lived waiting for the weekend, the year waiting for a holiday, and your lifespan waiting for retirement.

Work/life balance assumes that different aspects of your life are separate and competing, but also that some will be negative per se, and need to be balanced out.

We accept that the week isn't supposed to be fun, exercise isn't supposed to be enjoyable, learning isn't meant to be shared with others, and so it all needs to be balanced out. Looking for balance assumes the need for a compromise: that life is a zero-sum game, in which you will always have to make concessions and shortchange one area for another. Instead of maximising the positive aspects, balance focuses you on minimising the negatives. This is playing **not to lose**, instead of playing to win.

Instead of looking to counterbalance the negatives, go all in on all aspects of your life: focus on growing the entire sphere at the same time and become passionate about your entire 24 hours. When everything is aligned, it becomes effortless.

That's real balance: creating a life of passion, instead of managing the negatives, so you can fall in love with your every day.

When I started my first business, I went all in on it, thinking everything else will sort itself out once I got to some sort of "successful outcome." I put friends on pause and moved to another city, I stopped training and went to bed at random hours: after a few months, not only I felt stuck, I was also overworked and didn't have a structure to support me. My habits were poor, my friendships were weak, my health was shrinking, and I had to start from scratch—I was going bankrupt in almost every aspect of my life.

It's when I started looking after myself that things changed: investing in other people supported my growth, giving me confidence and opportunities; investing in my fitness increased my performance and resilience; taking time to learn new skills skyrocketed my results; and each aspect supported one another. Growth in each area was giving me the lessons and energy to grow in every other aspect. By compressing more into the same amount of time you will get more results and energy, perpetuating the positive cycle.

There are **three rules** to experience growth across your entire life sphere:

- *Your lowest standard is your standard*
- *Focus on managing energy, not time*
- *Align your activities to grow together*

Let's have a look at each one.

Your lowest standard is your standard

When you look at balance as a way to make the negative aspects of life bearable, you are constantly making compromises with yourself. That's the trap of work/life balance.

Pausing your fitness to focus on the "urgent" in your business means accepting a lower standard from yourself when it comes to health, performance, and even confidence.

Escaping an unfulfilling life through a two week holiday is a temporary band aid to make the everyday bearable, and to justifying some sort of compromise.

When you start dropping your standard in one area of your life, you will see your new, lowered expectations contaminate every other aspect.

Compromising on your social life will make you start compromising on your habits, your business performance or career, your relationships…and so on until it spreads to every other aspect of the life sphere. Your lower standard is your standard.

If something isn't working out in your life, the natural immediate response is to let go and deal with it later: remember, you are accumulating time debt (which you'll have to deal with in the future). Instead, embrace those areas that need work, and you'll see positive effects across your entire life.

Your life sphere is never stable: you can either grow it or let it shrink.

Manage energy

In the age of more, most people want to cram as much stuff as possible into their 24 hours: an infinite list of tasks leading to nowhere, flat social experiences that will be forgotten in a week, another audiobook that will never be actioned.

The myth of "hustle harder" holds back many people from creating their highest contribution: focusing them on what feels like the grind rather than prioritising what has the biggest impact. This focus on quantity rather than quality forgets that we only have 24 hours a day: **you cannot manage time**, but you can manage yourself in relation to time by choosing high-impact activities.

When you embrace all areas of life with passion and choose growth over compromise, you will suddenly have more energy and be able to do more. This is the real secret of high-performers. Think of a friend (or a celebrity) that seems to always be doing something cool, and manages to accomplish so much more than you in the same 24 hours: this is how they do it.

Compromises, and activities you get involved in because you tell yourself "you have to" drain your energy: you need to rest and recover from them afterwards.

Activities that bring growth and passion to your life are recharging and energising and will propel you forward throughout your day and your other commitments.

Having a full day of diverse activities is also a great way to stay high-energy and compress more into each day. For example, I love to alternate mentally challenging activities (like writing) with physically intense ones (like an explosive workout); or introverted occupations (like being in an office staring at a screen) with extroverted ones (such as going for a walk or meeting a group of people): that's how I keep filling up the tank and stay high energy throughout the day, every day.

That's another reason why you must embrace every aspect of life with the same intensity, even those that currently do not seem positive: striving for growth will give you a bigger battery to use in your everyday life. Instead of trying to manage time, manage your energy by focusing on high-impact activities that bring impact and growth.

Align your activities

When you see everything as separate, you miss the big picture. This is why getting a clear direction as we saw in chapter one, is so important to grow your life sphere, tap into that perpetual energy, and choose growth over compromise.

Looking at your life as made up of separate pieces makes it easy to get distracted and go in different, sidetracking directions. It becomes difficult to know what to say yes to, as we saw in the last chapter.

Having a clear purpose allows you to align all your activities and make progress across the board. Instead of saying yes to any opportunity that comes your way, you make sure that each one supports the rest and gets you closer to your goals.

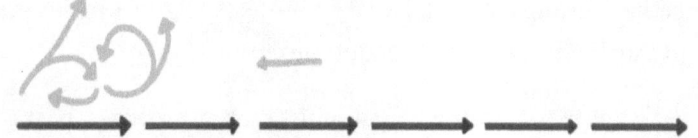

You can align anything, as long as it shares a common direction. For example, when I decided that I wanted to travel for extended periods of time, it forced me to align my business actions with my travel goals, and having that constraint ended up fuelling my business growth to the next stage.

A simple way to align your activities is sharing your life with others. Work/life balance has taught us to compartmentalise life and keep the pieces separate, including people most important to us. We do things in isolation, and then catch up over coffee to update each other on what happened in between coffee chats.

As a friend pointed out to me some time ago, that's why it's so much easier to build friendships in your younger years than in your adult life: by going through school and university, you share great, bonding experiences that get you closer. Later in life, we tend to catch up "outside" of our day-to-day life, which makes it slow and more challenging to create shared memories and experiences that grow a strong human connection.

The secret to aligning is to share your life with others: from learning a language or a new skill together, to travelling to a new country for a great experience, all the way to supporting each other's business activities (and tough challenges).

This has worked wonders in my life: I used to do everything on my own and struggled to find the time for great relationships. It's when I started to share my workouts, writing sessions, meals, walks, and travels with the people in my life and business, that's when things really took off.

By sharing openly, you will create experiences that are part of your life, not separate from it. As a result, you won't have to juggle separate things, and your relationships will grow stronger and stronger by sharing moments and activities.

When everything fits in the same picture, you no longer have to juggle. You don't have to prioritise work or life (or any aspect of it), because it's all the same.

That's the power of aligning your commitments and going all in on everything.

What now

Time to take action and close things that are not serving the big picture.

In the last chapter, you learned about a great process you can use to focus on what brings you results and say no to everything else; in chapter eleven, we will go through a simple test to see whether something fits in your future or not, whether it's worth your time or not.

Make sure that everything is aligned in your life and supports everything else.

When you align, you can manage energy instead of trying (and failing) to manage time.

For now, as you go through your day, make a mental note of all those commitments that are not serving your bigger picture, those acts that are lowering your standard and expectations, and even slowly eroding your identity: is it adding to your life or subtracting?

When you say no to what doesn't fit the big picture, that's when you can quit juggling.

CHAPTER FIVE
LIFE-CHANGING DAILY ACTIONS

Whatever you practice, you get good at."

Denzel Washington

If you are sitting down while reading this, your hamstrings, the muscles that attach to the back of your knees, are slowly shortening. If you spend most of your day sitting down, your body will adapt to be great at sitting.

We constantly adapt, both physically and mentally, to become great at responding to our environment and challenges (while minimising the need for resources like calories and energy).

If you start training like an athlete, your body and muscles will adapt to respond to physical demands. Likewise, if you stop training and spend your days on the couch, your body will adapt and change your body composition, as well as your energy levels and metabolism[10].

There's no quick switch: your daily actions will determine whether you become an athlete or a world-class couch potato.

This applies to every aspect of life: business, career, nutrition, relationships, fulfilment...what you decide to practice today trains you to do more of the same tomorrow. Even if you don't do anything, you are teaching yourself how to be great at putting off taking action.

I used to behave like life has a pause button: for a year, I paused my fitness training, my friendships, and my relationship, and went all in on my business instead.

I thought I could pick them up later and get it all back on track in no time. A few months passed, and I had to start from scratch in all those areas: I was incredibly skinny, and most of my friendships had withered, along with most other aspects of my life.

Together with thinking we can pause things without seeing any change, most of us are convinced that positive change requires a lot of work at once: go hard or go home.

The problem with this approach is that it requires a big commitment, going for sudden radical change instead of working your way towards new, sustainable results. Typically,

---

[10] Eric T. Trexler, Abbie E. Smith-Ryan, Layne E. Norton, *Metabolic adaptation to weight loss: implications for the athlete*, 2014

you start with a lot of motivation, only to see it fizzle out when things get difficult after a few days or weeks once the first real challenges present themselves. This is also why almost 90% of New Year's resolutions are abandoned within a few months[11].

Going for quick bursts is the equivalent of walking into the gym for the first time in your life and attempting to squat 200kg: you'd get yourself injured and would never want to go back again.

We underestimate what we can accomplish with tiny daily actions, and overestimate what we can accomplish in occasional bursts.

The power of 1% better

Tiny daily actions are the key to big, sustained results: whatever you practice, you get good at. It's tempting to go for big, radical change. For example, restructure your entire day and go from reading zero books to aiming for 2 a month. But that never lasts, and you're left with a 0% improvement.

Choosing to get 1% better every day, on the other hand, is a much more manageable endeavour. It requires a small commitment that can be sustained over time.

---

[11] Norcross, John & S Mrykalo, Marci & D Blagys, Matthew. (2002). Auld Lang Syne: Success Predictors, Change Processes, and Self-Reported Outcomes of New Year's Resolvers and Nonresolvers. Journal of clinical psychology. 58. 397-405. 10.1002/jclp.1151.

Let's take reading as an example: you decide you want to read more. So you get a ton of books just in case, and decide to go from barely a book a year to reading three a month. After all, you've changed.

Except, two weeks later you haven't finished a single chapter and decide to give up. You went from zero books a year to zero books a year. The only difference is that now you are disappointed in yourself and don't have confidence in your abilities. You were better off before the experiment.

If, on the other hand, you decided to read two pages every day, that would add up to 730 pages a year, which is about 4 books. By taking on a small, very sustainable commitment, you have gone from zero books to four books. Doubling it next time will be a total breeze. The secret is to make your actions **excuse-proof**.

Another reason why tiny actions are easier to keep up is that they can be done every single day. Or at least, they can be predictably added to your calendar. When you read two pages every day at the same time, you create an automatic habit. Instead of having to decide to read and then figure out the mechanics of the when, where, and what, you just decide to let your **daily habit** guide you.

A habit is a regular practice which is actually stored in a different part of the brain (the basal ganglia) responsible for automatic response and motor movement. It bypasses your conscious control, making sure you do the right thing on autopilot.

Committing to doing something daily or on a schedule also changes **your identity**: it becomes who you are, not just what you do.

Why do some people only eat vegetarian food, and consistently stick to avoiding meat? Their stomach is exactly the same as everyone else's, but their beliefs and identity are different.

That's the power of shifting your identity: when you change who you are first, how you act will become a simple byproduct of it. But when you never shape your identity and let others decide it for you, it becomes nearly impossible to change your actions.

When you look beyond their immediate impact, tiny daily actions are extremely powerful. While big bursts leave you high and dry, tiny actions taken consistently can carry you to big results in every area of your life. The reason? Simple math.

Compound results

If you buy a coffee a day for $2.99, in a year you'll have spent $1,091. Let's call it $1,000.

Now, say that you pay for those coffees using a credit card that has 0% interest rate for the first year. At the end of the first year, you'll have accumulated $1,000 debt.

Let's imagine that you keep your balance and for the next 10 years, you pay a 10% annual interest rate.

After a year, you'll owe the bank $1,100.

After five years, you'll owe $1,610.51.

After ten, that'll be $2,593.74.

Notice anything?

On the first year of 10% interest, you accumulated an extra $100. However, on the tenth year that has grown to an extra $235 for that year alone. Growth on growth has made that annual interest skyrocket to way more than double.

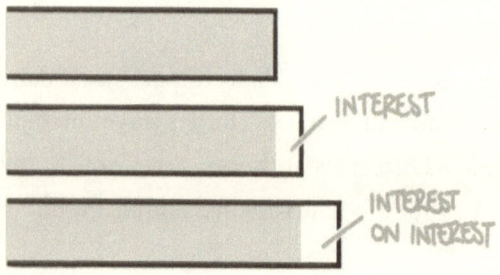

The reason why your interest increases every year is the principle that banks and investors use to generate money from an initial deposit: compound interest.

Compound interest is essentially **interest on interest**: any percentage increment affects the previous increments too. Think of this as some sort of snowball effect in digits.

The power of compound interest applies to **tiny daily actions** too. Becoming 1% better every day will only give you marginal gains each single day. You probably won't even notice them.

But here's the cool thing, that 1% will compound on your previous gains, increasing your progress *exponentially*.

Keep your tiny efforts up for 365 days, and you won't get 365% better—you will get 3,800%. That's 38 times better, in just a year.

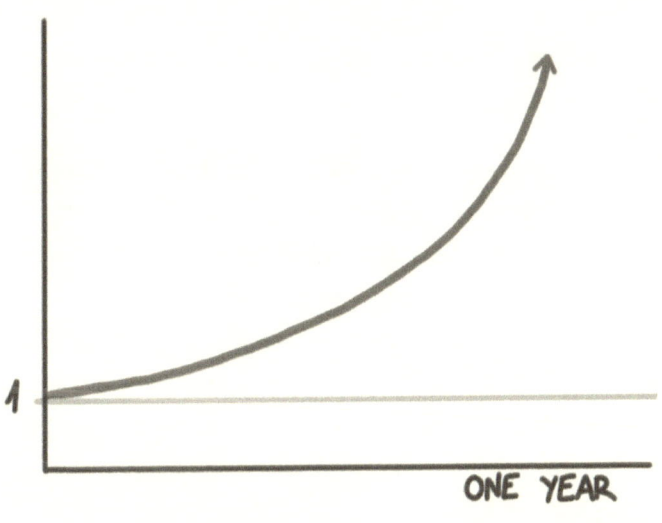

This is why tiny actions are so much more powerful than occasional bursts: you can accomplish so much more through consistent, small action, while sporadic sprints leave you tired and deflated.

You can take a whole weekend off and read one book. That's still one book a year.

Or you can read 2 pages a day, and that's 4 books a year.

You can go to a three day conference as a one-off and meet 8 people.

Or you can organise a coffee chat with a new person a week, and meet 52 people.

You can dedicate two weeks to writing your book, and stay stuck on the first chapter.

Or you can write 450 words a day, and publish two books in a year.

I like to be very intentional with my 1%, and also make it fun: focus on things that recharge me and break up my workload. For example, I learned to sketchnote by drawing for 10 minutes every morning while taking a break from work. That way, I was able to split my workload in two while learning and having fun. With a minimum commitment I was able to radically improve my sketching abilities almost effortlessly, all while making my day more sustainable and my productivity higher.

Here are some of my favourite examples of tiny actions that bring you disproportionate results (but feel free to create your own to support your own growth):

- *Reading two pages of a book a day*
- *Doing a five minute tabata workout every morning*

- *Meditating or doing guided breathing for 3 minutes*
- *Writing 300 words every day towards your book*
- *Learning a fundamental skill like sketching or touch typing*
- *Doing dual n back memory training for 5 minutes[12]*

Tiny actions are a great way to face things that you know are important but don't feel like are a priority right now. You either want to pause them or constantly feel that "you don't have the time" (by now, you know that's an excuse). Tiny actions are a way to make constant progress while on autopilot, with a very manageable commitment.

To make sure you stick to your tiny action, it's important to keep it small, resist the temptation to add too many at once, and appreciate small progress (so you don't give up).

---

[12] *Working memory training improves emotional states of healthy individuals*, 2014

Appreciate small progress

In the age of instant gratification and immediate communication, we expect results to show up immediately.

Yet, that's not the natural progression of things. Any growth is usually made of a decision to start, a process of adjustment and progress, and lastly the final accomplishment.

When we don't appreciate progress, we tend to go back to the start: it's like we'd rather have zero progress than SOME progress.

I worked with an entrepreneur who went to bed past 4am every night. Work, thoughts, and finally a sense of disappointment in his day kept him up till the wee small hours of the morning. Every day, he'd wake up at the most random times and do it all over again.

To stop the root of the problem, we restructured his daily habits and workload so that he could go to bed earlier. Our final aim was to work our way to an average 11pm bedtime. When we checked in after the first week, he sounded so disappointed in himself: he had gone to bed at 1am every night. In his eyes, it was a total failure, until I pointed out that he'd just adjusted his personal time zone by 3 hours, and we were over 50% of the way to our goal in just a few days. By looking at what was working instead of what was lacking, we were able to continue and get to our final result, instead of giving up more than halfway through.

Noticing progress is like seeing a child grow: from a parent's point of view (or the child's), nothing ever happens until you look at a picture and...you notice how much they have changed. For everyone else seeing the child once every few months though, it's a shock each time.

Change is only evident from a distance.

To appreciate small, constant progress, don't wait for results to stare in your face: design a way to keep track.

If your goal is measurable, track one metric: how many books you read, or how many words you can type per minute.

If your goal is visual, compare what you can see: you can take pictures of your fitness progress, or collect your sketches to see how much you've improved.

Just don't leave it to chance.

1% worse every day

We're always training, remember? So does compound interest apply to letting things go too? The answer is, of course, yes.

Nothing stays constant: you're either growing or shrinking.

So when you decide not to face a particular fear, or to leave a specific area of your life on hold, here's what will happen: you will adapt to become worse in that area, or better at giving in to that fear holding back.

The same happens when you pick up a negative action, like smoking or eating junk food regularly: your body is constantly responding and slowly getting worse.

If you can't notice that change happening, it's for the same reason why it's difficult to see progress: change is difficult to spot, unless you're distant from it.

In the meantime, you keep getting imperceptibly worse. Let's say it's 1% worse every day: how does the compound

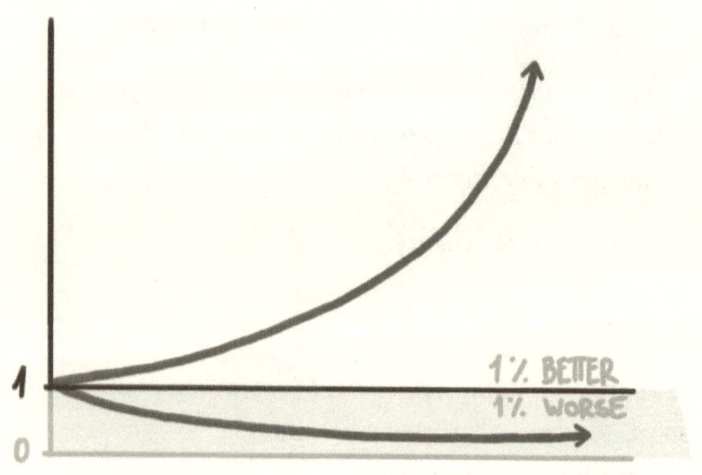

effect work then?

1% worse every day will leave you with only 3% of your initial resources left after a single year. That's the 1% rule: if you do something daily, you will see big results, whether positive or negative (you decide).

As you move in either direction, the change is too small and constant for you to notice: it's easy to ignore it and not fully understand the impact of how much you are adapting to what's happening around you.

If you're learning a new skill, like drawing, tiny increments are difficult to notice.

If you're letting an area of life get out of control, like taking care of your relationships, the slow burn will be tough to spot.

But once you stop and look back, everything has changed. If you let things erode, it will take you a massive amount of time to get back where you were; if you accumulated a new win, all you have to do is stick to those tiny actions to stay strong and keep growing.

The key is to learn to appreciate progress. Be intentional and choose to put constant effort towards what's important to you. Compound interest will do the rest for you.

I can't wait to see what you accomplish a year from today.

What now

The first step to mastering the power of compound interest is to stop the negative behaviours that are making you 1% worse every day and slowly eating away at your strengths.

What **negative behaviours** do you have on a regular basis? Smoking, binge eating, junk food, staying stuck in the sleepless cycle…all these are examples of choices that, as a one-off can be fine and even enjoyable, but when kept up regularly slowly erode your baseline and your ability to live a full life.

What **areas of life** are you negating? Remember what you learned in the last chapter about balance: the more you look at life as made up of separate things you can "juggle," the more you will struggle and get exhausted, instead of living a full life of constant growth.

If there's anything you are ignoring in life, remember that it's affecting everything else and holding you back from your potential. Align your actions so they all work with each other.

Next, you can look for things you want to **add to your life**, like a skill or a mindset.

Once you've identified what needs your attention, break that down into small tiny action: what would slowly get you to your result if you show up daily?

The last step is to create a way to take action every day: this could be booking a daily slot in your calendar, creating a reminder on your phone, or having a set of actions you take every day. Remember to be specific as to what's the minimum requirement for your action: when does it start? When does it end? Knowing what is enough will help you keep your commitment small and excuse-proof.

Remember to download your free worksheet, so you can keep taking action as you read through the book.

timezillionaire.com/invest-bonus

In the next chapter, we will see how you can create systems that automatically support your goals and actions, so you can make progress without even having to think about it.

CHAPTER SIX
THE STRUCTURE TO BE UNSTRUCTURED

"Discipline is freedom."

Jocko Willink

Some things are in our control and others not.

Focusing on the things you cannot influence brings stress; focusing on the things you can influence brings power.

The definition of stress is "pressure or tension exerted on a material object": when you want things to be different, you create that tension between how you want things to be and how things really are.

Shunning any sort of structure in your life means giving up your power, while wishing for the things you cannot control to be different.

That's why the most structured people really are the most flexible, while the most unstructured ones are locked into unchanging conditions. The first ones manage circumstances, the second ones are managed by them.

For example, most of my mornings look the same: wake up at a set time, train or meditate for one hour, journal, play some music and do a little dance, take a cold shower, have breakfast, and set my intention for the day. I know exactly when my morning routine starts, when it ends, and how I'm going to feel by the end of it.

When I casually mention this in a first conversation with a stranger, the most common reaction is "you are so structured," followed by them telling me how they could never have a morning routine and how they do everything last minute. Some feel compelled to let me know how they would "get bored of things being so predictable."

What they fail to realize is that having reliable structure allows me to ground myself and get the important done everyday, so I can enjoy as much flexibility as I can outside of that.

In the meantime, they are the ones living the regimented life: these comments often come from people that have to be in the same office on set times (even when the sun is shining), spend their weekends doing a different version of the same thing, and only take occasional travel breaks to predictable destinations.

This is being unstructured in the small things that make no difference, and giving up control on the big picture: what actually matters.

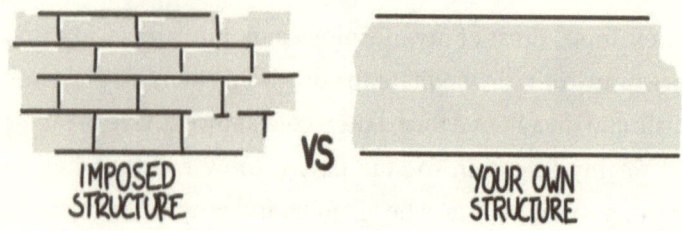

In chapter three, we met Decision Fatigue, a cognitive limitation that deteriorates the quality of our decision-making throughout the day: the more decisions we take, the more our willpower and ability to decide rationally fades away. In the age of infinite (petty) choices, we are constantly faced with micro decisions that have no impact on our lives.

Small decisions give us the illusion of flexibility and spontaneity, but it comes at the cost of being unable to make big choices that shape the direction of our lives. So we end up not choosing.

Not choosing is a choice

Life is like moving down a river: we can't change the speed or direction, and we can't decide where each split in the river will take us: but we can choose which one to pick. Over time, those choices shape our lives.

Most of our everyday conditions are outside of our control. The people we meet, the information we come across, the language and culture we are exposed to, other people's reactions, the weather, the films available to us. And for those conditions we have power of choice over, most of the time we still do not control the set of choices available to us.

Focusing on what you can't influence gives you a feeling of blamelessness: the illusion that by focusing on the small things and avoiding those big, significant decisions, you are not to blame for what happens next.

But choosing not to choose is still a clear choice. There's no stopping the flow of events of life: instead of choosing which split in the river you want to go down, you decide to let randomness take control for you. It's still your decision to do so.

Not choosing is a choice. Not quitting a job is choosing to stay in a job. Not breaking up with someone is choosing to give more time to that relationship. Not launching a new product or starting a new adventure is choosing to give up on your dreams.

By letting go of your power, you also allow yourself to feel like a victim of circumstances and be off the hook: there's nothing you can do about it.

When you take on responsibility instead, and make meaningful choices, you take on the ability to respond to circumstances. When you choose and take action, you can then see what happens next and adjust. But when you give up the power of choice, that's when you get stuck, not knowing what to do next.

When you choose not to choose, it's impossible to invest your time: instead of stacking positive actions that will cumulate and create ripple effects in your present and future, you take small, insignificant decisions that keep you bogged down living the same day, every day.

You can manage circumstances or be managed by them. Either way, **it's your choice**.

The myth of being spontaneous

At a speaking event, someone asked me: "How can I combine being a creative with the structure of running a business?"

The question assumed that structure and creativity are enemies, when in fact they are best friends: structure shields your creative endeavours from constant interruptions.

Similarly, many people fight any sort of planning or structure with the idea of wanting to be spontaneous, deciding in the moment, and capturing the opportunities that life sends their way.

The definition of spontaneous is something "performed or occurring as a result of a sudden impulse or inclination and without premeditation or external stimulus."

Being in the moment is amazing: instead of waiting for a later time, you fully enjoy the present, right now.

But the value of being spontaneous depends on the circumstances you have: one day, I decided to call my landlord, move out of my flat, and fly to Portugal for a month. I ended up travelling for 6 months. That was pretty spontaneous, yet a lot had to happen behind the scenes to make it possible: I created a business that allowed me to travel and work remotely; I perfected daily rituals which allowed me to live and perform anywhere on any day; I systematically did something uncomfortable every week, which enabled me to take such a scary step without too much thinking.

The choice was spontaneous, but the circumstances that allowed that choice were designed.

For example, I only take coaching calls on Monday afternoons and Thursdays. That created a big constraint to the initial growth of my business, and it also means that those two days are super fulfilling...but also <u>very</u> intense. However, this structure allows me to take Tuesday morning off and have breakfast with a friend, or fly out on Wednesday to work from abroad for a week.

Structure enables me to be unstructured.

Whether you want to go to the gym in the middle of the afternoon, say yes to playing poker with friends on a Wednesday night, go on a long walk during the day, or take even bigger, spontaneous decisions, the ability to do so comes from being able to design your circumstances.

Otherwise, being spontaneous becomes a mere excuse: a cop out from taking big decisions that would create actual results, or a way to rationalise decision fatigue after a day of meaningless choices. When you use spontaneity as an excuse, you end up spending time on the unimportant, constantly too tired to actually spend time on what matters to you.

Instead of creating meaningful moments and truly living the present, you end up doing the same things over and over again, while you order the same takeaway food you had last Friday.

Constant spontaneity shuns any kind of constraints: but how can you experience true freedom if you have nothing to be free from? Just like darkness needs the absence of light to exist (and vice versa), so it is for freedom and constraints.

When you constantly reject constraints and barriers, you end up working within the ones that someone else decides for you. That's why designing your own structure is so powerful: you can use them to create systems and barriers that guide you towards the freedom you truly desire, not just that are available to you. When you design a structure that works for you, it empowers you to make the most of every moment in your day, be truly spontaneous, and see compound results over time. So you can invest your time.

A system working for you

A system is *"a set of principles or procedures according to which something is done; an organized scheme or method."*

Systems allow you to have a reliable structure working for you instead of having to do everything from scratch every single time. This allows you to reduce the amount of daily choices, cognitive load, and ultimately decision fatigue.

Without systems, you will spend most of your time deciding on things that are either irrelevant or repeating, like "What do I want to have for lunch today?" You'll have no time and no headspace left to think about the big things that matter, like "What job do I want? Which skill do I want to learn next?"

Instead of taking insignificant microdecisions all the time, you create principles that apply every single time without fail: it may take you a little bit longer at the start to figure it out, but you will get disproportionate results in terms of flexibility and growth.

And since structures don't need to be redesigned and thought out every time, they can be optimised, automated, and even outsourced and given to someone else.

That's **the structure to be unstructured**: by creating constraints and processes in your life and business, you can focus and see real progress when you want to, so you can relax and be spontaneous when you don't want to.

Systems empower you not to be on all the time, and that's why things work for you.

Here are some of my favourite systems you can implement starting from this week:

A system around what you eat.

What did you have for lunch two days ago?

Chances are, you have no idea. Yet, most of us approach it as a new decision every day: browsing the supermarket aisle, or walking through the food court, we wonder "What do I feel like today?" Not only is that an irrelevant decision with no lasting effects, it gives up on the bigger picture: the ability to decide what foods you want to impact your chemistry and body composition. After all, what you eat today is what you will be made of tomorrow.

A meal plan is a system, and so is batch cooking. By deciding what you are going to eat during the day in advance (and possibly cooking it too), you can lump a number of everyday decisions into a weekly one. This also allows you to follow your principles and goals, instead of becoming the victim of cravings and decision fatigue.

A dietary restriction is a system. When you decide to cut out something from your menu, you create a system on how to choose. You may be on a high-fat diet, or cutting out foods you are sensitive to, or avoiding foods that cause your afternoon slump: when you decide on a principle, you reduce your menu of daily choices and stick to your good decisions on autopilot.

A system allows you to make great decisions automatically every day, so you can go all in and truly enjoy memorable foods when you actually decide to. Guilt free.

A system to take control of your time.

Trusting your calendar fully is a system. Blocking time for a particular task is a system. Spending the first hour of your morning writing is a system. When it comes to mastering your time, using constraints, being specific and intentional, and putting yourself in your own agenda are the most important ingredients to creating systems you can rely on.

In the next chapter, we will go through how to take control of your week, so you can create a system for what really matters to you (and stop procrastinating).

A system to learn more.

Deciding to read a book, take a course, or learn a new skill is a commitment. It's easy to start enthusiastically, only to see that motivation taper off and disappear as daily obligations get in the way.

Deciding to read one page every day is a system. Leaving your book on the kitchen table and booking 20m daily in your calendar is a system. So is listening to an audiobook on your drive to work. Instead of deciding daily and scrambling to "find the time," you decide once and for all and let the decision take care of your action.

A system to work out.

Just like learning, regularly working out is much easier if you have a system to follow.

The system could be a training plan, telling you exactly what to do and on which day. Having a fixed appointment with the gym (or, even better, with a gym buddy) on set days during the week is a system. Having a weekly workout target is a system.

Training is the ultimate analogy for any meaningful growth in life: you show up, you see nothing but pain, you keep showing up, you finally see results. Having a system to trust and take away discrete decisions allows you to continue progressing, even when all you want to do is give up.

A system to grow your business.

When you run a business, it feels like you have to do everything: the first thing I did when I came up with my first business idea was to buy a domain and open every single social media account. Genius. As an entrepreneur, there is so much you could do, and there's always a better tactic: it's exhausting and it requires a ton of attention.

Instead, having a clear goal for every different area of your business (such as product development, sales, and operations), and then breaking each down into actions you can complete and measure, creates a system you can follow without having to think everything from scratch every time. Even better if you assign a specific time to each major action, as we will see in the next chapter. A system takes care of the mechanics, so you are free to work your magic.

A system to get uncomfortable.

Leaving your comfort zone is something everyone talks about, but very few people do. That's because we are wired to stay comfortable and stick to what we know: unless you actively look for growth experiences, you will keep postponing them.

That's why, a few years back, my friend Phil and I decided to keep each other accountable to doing one uncomfortable thing every week. From giving flowers to a stranger to bungee jumping, all the way to cutting a barber's hair in his own shop, training myself to feel comfortable with rejection and fear helped me get ready to make difficult life decisions. Without it,

I don't think I would have ever taken the risk to go on my first extended travels and bring my life and business to 6 countries over 6 months.

Having a list of challenges, someone to keep me accountable, and a weekly cadence was the system that allowed me to leave my comfort zone for good.

A system for your team.

Going from a one-person band to having a team or working with contractors is a tough transition. The usual reaction is to keep all control and give out tasks: the challenge with that is that now there is more you have to decide on. It's like multiplying your arms and your hours, but having the same one brain to do it all.

In the meantime, the team feels directionless and has no room to manoeuvre.

When I coach business owners on how to go through such a transformation, the first thing we work on is getting everyone on the same page when it comes to defined roles and clear goals; the second thing is setting a system to take care of communication.

Knowing who calls the shots on what (and why), having a clear way to share progress on your goals (without having to ask for it), and encouraging communication (both positive and negative), is difficult to implement without a system everyone can trust and rely upon.

A system to create great experiences.

I have a friend who schedules a date with himself every month. One month, he took himself to paint in the park. Another month, he went to explore a new city nearby. Another time, he just went to the best coffee shop in London and read a book for 4 hours.

Though it sounded odd at first, I love the idea: when you rely on spontaneous, you tend to go for the usual options, and put yourself after everyone else.

Even for those of us privileged enough to have the flexibility of working flexible hours remotely, the option of creating amazing experiences isn't worth anything unless you use it.

My friend Rich found himself working from home most of the time: when cabin fever became too much, he decided to work from a new location every Wednesday and invite people to join him. Not only he had a system to leave the house, he also had one to meet new people to work and do business with.

Working from a different place once a week, and inviting two friends to join, is a system.

Having an email to remind you to do something totally new every week (I like to use fut.io to get reminders in my inbox) is a system, and so is blocking a time in your calendar to make sure you get out of the house.

What now

Systems and principles allow real freedom: by creating universal guidelines that take care of all small decisions on your behalf, you can make progress on autopilot and save your resources for high-impact, life-changing decisions. This will also reduce your stress, as you don't have to constantly think about every single moving part of your life, and you don't have to constantly "find the time" to do what matters. Trust the system and good things will happen.

When you don't design your own structure, you will fall victim to someone else's. Through advertising, social conventions, and individual expectations, other people will design ways to shortcut your "spontaneous" decisions when you don't have a system to support your values and direction and shield you from decision fatigue.

Having a structure that works for you also allows you to deviate from the main path whenever you want to: you will confidently know how, when, and by whom everything important will be taken care of, so you can be present and enjoy truly spontaneous activities.

Designing constraints is the ultimate freedom.

Now that you are familiar with systems, in the next chapter I will walk you through the details of mapping out your entire week and rapidly planning your day in advance, so you can start to rely on a proven system in your life and business.

CHAPTER SEVEN
HOW TO OWN YOUR 24 HOURS

"Every battle is won or lost before it is ever fought."

Sun Tzu

When we think about budgets, money is the first thing that comes to mind: how much is going in and out over a set period of time, and how to manage that flow.

However, money isn't finite, nor scarce: you can always make more money. If you've ever had a promotion, a new job, a new product launch, or found a better client, then you know that the amount of money you can make is not fixed. It's also renewable. If your bank account gets dangerously close to overdraft on the last week of the month, you know your next salary will soon come in to give you some respite. In a business, you can find more clients or sell a new product to existing customers to regenerate and even expand your cash flow.

While most resources are renewable, time isn't one of them: once you have experienced an hour, there's no way to get that time back. It's gone <u>forever</u>.

Sure, every day we get 24 more hours, but our days are limited, and they can't be traded nor renewed: time is the only truly limited resource.

It's also the one every other resource depends upon: whether you want to expand your business, meet more people, create a new product, or learn a new skill, you will need to invest your time to do so. Money can shortcut that process, but it can't extend your time.

While only ⅓ of people keep a regular budget for their money[13], almost no one allocates their time intentionally. Yet, time is finite and can be used to create more money, while the opposite isn't true. Companies and governments can become obsessed budgeting large sums of money, and totally ignore the large sums of time their organisation handles collectively.

This assumes that time has some sort of intrinsic value: that each minute is worth the same as any other. As we saw in chapter one, time does not have a constant value. In fact, it has

---

[13] Dennis Jacobe, *One in Three Americans Prepare a Detailed Household Budget*, 2013

no value per se: it's what you do with and experience in that time that creates any value for yourself and others.

Spend your whole week working in a job you hate, or mindlessly watching the same tv show (while the food stains accumulate on your shirt), and pretty soon you'll hate yourself. Guaranteed.

But experience a week of challenging growth, passionate work, great moments shared with friends, and you'll become obsessed about wanting to create more of that.

Plus, the results will compound, making each week even better than the previous one.

Owning your 24 hours means being intentional with how you allocate your time across your most important experiences, projects, and creation of other resources: in previous chapters, we learned how compounding actions, investing your time, and managing energy actually create disproportionate results with your time, which you can then use to increase the impact of it. If you don't shape your 24 hours, someone else will do it for you.

Most people organise their time around what they think is expected of them, including:

- *Activities they hate (e.g. tidying up the house or cooking)*
- *Activities that include other people (e.g. meeting that friend constantly in need of attention)*
- *Recurring duties and events (e.g. work)*

Any remaining time is for them to use, if any is left.

Now the issue is that the little time left is chopped up in small bits between the "others" events, and often so short it's difficult to allocate in any meaningful way.

The second challenge is that often this time is very undesirable: it comes after every other duty and commitment, and often means that your energy levels, motivation, and energy are very, very low. An excellent example of the value of time not being constant.

In other words, you are left with the leftovers of your day, starving yourself of any possibility of accomplishment and growth after having fed everyone else. This keeps you repeating the same things while waiting for results to change over time, while the only guarantee is that you'll get older in the meantime.

Organizing your time has a negative connotation: from school time to the 9-5, other people create a structure for us without even explaining why. So we refuse to take any control over our own time: rejecting any form of planning feels rebellious, and almost freeing from constraints.

But by refusing to create a structure that works for us, we can never break away from those imposed externally: instead of managing our day, we let it manage us.

This attitude fails to question the impact of giving your time indiscriminately to anyone that demands it. The fallacy is the old one: giving time an intrinsic value, and therefore going for quantity over quality. By now you know that the only thing that matters is how much value your create with your 24 hours in terms of resources, experiences, and skills.

The only way to be able to offer more to yourself and the important people in your life is to go beyond time and increase the value you can generate with each day. Your time does not matter: what you create for yourself and others with it does. And the only way to increase this is to intentionally invest your time, and allocate regular slots to activities that keep giving you compound results in the future and inspire others to do the same.

Some time ago, a friend texted me out of the blue, saying "Thank you so much: I just got a raise and it's thanks to your example and your advice." Reading it felt amazing. Even more so considering that I had only seen this person twice over the previous two years. Yet, we made that count: it's not about how much time. In fact, it's not quantity that matters, but quality: the value that you generate and how much you can grow any relationship in a given time.

The difficult piece of news is that you are going to have to choose what to focus on, and you may have to drop what does not move the needle. Go back to the exercise in chapter one, where you wrote down your future direction: where you want your life to be 3-5 years from today.

Now it's time to expand that, and **write a list of activities** you have on right now. Next to each, estimate how much time you think you spend on each per week. Be totally honest with yourself. Then, reconcile that list with the 3-5 year vision you wrote at the start of the book: which activities are supporting that goal? Which will be there in the future?

Eliminate the ones that don't pass the test (you may have already done this in chapter four, well done if so).

Then, the next step is to **track your time** for at least two weeks.

You can use a spreadsheet, a piece of paper, a time-tracking app, or any other way that works for you. The important thing is that you record how you spend your time in one-hour increments, and think back on your day at least twice a day.

The last step is to then **compare** your initial list with your actual time spent: prepare yourself to be shocked.

Now that we've reached awareness, it's time to move onto using your calendar for yourself.

How to map your time

I used to remember every single appointment in my weekly schedule. If someone asked me, "Are you free on Tuesday?" I would immediately know what was expecting me on that particular day and for the rest of the week. Until I realised three things:

1. This made me pretty reactive, looking for "empty spots" in my calendar instead of looking at the whole picture.

2. As my level of activity increased, it became clear that I just couldn't keep up with all the complexity without a system.

3. Having to remember my commitments was taking up precious mental energy that I could have allocated in a different way.

That's when I started to rely on my calendar, with one rule only: "the calendar never lies."

In fact, if you are going to use a system, it's important that you trust it fully: allow it to do its thing, so you can focus on something else.

Using your calendar, agenda, or a system to map out your time will allow you to be in control of the bigger picture: instead of only considering events that include others or that you must do, you can start to allocate time to everything that really matters.

From growth activities to "me time," all the way to work sprints and shared experiences, you can adopt the only kind of meeting that will change your life: the one with yourself.

Here are a few quick techniques you can use to get back in control of your time.

Quick Day Planning (QDP)

Planning your day in advance is the quickest way to claim ownership over your 24 hours: it only takes a few minutes, and can literally change your day, every day.

Having a clear day plan shields you from getting distracted by external requests and getting lost in an infinite list of tasks that have no clear direction (and are often in competition).

To create your day plan, you'll need either a piece of paper or a digital note (separate from your messy to-do list): you want to start fresh, and without any constraints. Here's how to quickly plan your day following the QDP structure:

STEP #1: Look at your calendar, and write down any events you have on for the day. This will allow you to better gauge how much time you have available for your tasks.

STEP #2: Look at your current goals, and identify **one daily objective** that will get you closer to them. This is not one thing you can start, but rather one you will finish today. It needs to have a clear start, a clear action, and a clear end, all today. This step will ensure that you keep making progress and don't get distracted by an overwhelming list of tasks or sidetracked by events and external distractions.

STEP #3: only at this point, you can look at your to-dos. You can select 2-5 big tasks, depending on how much time other events will be taking from your day. When selecting 5, prioritise the most important two, and only then move on to the final three.

The QDP technique allows you to take control of your day within minutes, and ensures that you will make constant progress while at the same time managing circumstances (instead of being managed by them).

The fundamental principle behind this technique is the **reverse pyramid**: instead of starting from the many tasks that don't get you anywhere (but make you feel like you are getting a lot done, though it's all irrelevant), you start from the few, big tasks that may be uncomfortable but will guarantee you have a great day right from the start. Follow this principle, and you will make serious progress by lunchtime, every day.

I recommend planning your next day at the end of your work day, before you go home or switch to a personal activity: this allows you to start the day fresh and with clear priorities. However, if for whatever reason you cannot plan your next day last thing, you can have it as part of your morning ritual (you could pair it with breakfast or journalling).

Plan your week in advance

A more sophisticated way to organise the time available to you is to plan your week in advance. This is not for the beginner, so make sure you get used to relying on your calendar and planning your day with the QDP method first.

When you're ready to step things up, it's time to look at the week as a whole. I used to do this every Sunday, until I merged it with my admin block (more in the next section) on Friday afternoon. It takes me about one hour, but it saves me days (and eventually even months) down the line. In fact, the first thing to do when starting to plan your week is to decide when you are going to do it: if you don't, you'll be tempted to keep putting this off until…well, the week has either started or it's over. We are going to plan in advance, remember?

The first step is to **review the previous week**. You can do this by looking at your calendar, your completed tasks and objectives, and your time tracker if you're using one.

This is important because it will give you an opportunity to reflect on the week, notice what didn't take you anywhere, and do better next week. By looking back on your previous week, you can do more of what works and less of what doesn't (and identify what's stealing your time).

The second step is to **look at your objectives** and deadlines coming up.

You want to break down your overall objectives (for the quarter or year) into weekly milestones, starting with the end in mind: work backwards from the end, and create measurable weekly milestones that will ensure you will eventually hit your goal.

That way, when you plan your week, all you have to do is look for the next step forward and assign it to a specific day. Then do the same for deadlines coming up.

The third step is to **look at events** for the week. You want to do three things: understand what's ahead; eliminate what does not align with your objectives; add what is missing that will support them. Remember: it's ok to add yourself to your own calendar.

At this point, if you work with a team, you want to check their commitments, deadlines, and work, in order to sync up.

Finally, the last step is to **batch tasks** that are similar in nature, so you can deal with them at the same time: batching allows you to focus on fewer things at any one time, optimise processes, and eliminate duplicate work. It also limits task switching, keeping your attention focused on a single thing, making you faster and more effective.

That's why you'll love the next section on how to theme your days, the ultimate way to batch what matters to you.

Once you have your one objective and deadlines, a list of batched tasks, and a clear idea of the events ahead, all you have to do is to spread these **across the week** according to time available, priorities, and themes. That way, you will have an even week that allows you to work on everything that is important, instead of constantly having to sprint and juggle.

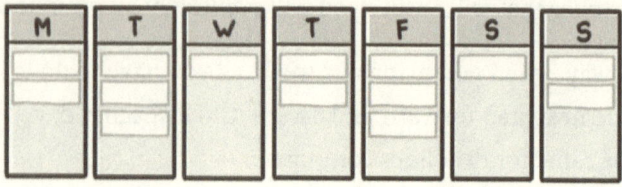

Theme your days

Theming is a powerful tool based on the concept of batching.

Essentially, you find the most important recurring themes in your life and work, and assign them to a particular day (or half day) of the week. For example, I like to write on Monday and Tuesday morning, while I plan my week and take care of recurring admin on Friday afternoon. Having a theme allows you to know when a specific kind of task will be done, but also (perhaps, more importantly) when it will not be done.

By creating a sacred space for recurring activities that are important, you make sure you always set aside enough time for them, in spite of "urgent" activities that may get in the way.

For example, if your admin theme is Friday afternoon (like me-yay!), you can batch admin emails and tasks and keep them waiting until Friday. That way, you will have the peace of mind of knowing exactly when it will happen, while at the same time avoiding present interruptions.

If you work with a team, it's important that you share your themes and restrictions with them: not only might they be inspired to do the same and become more efficient (and less stressed), they also are able to sync up with you and know exactly what to expect.

You can all set parallel themes that require you to work individually (so you know not to interrupt each other), and leave the rest to collaborate.

Communication is key if you want to stick to and get results from your themes.

Time blocks and the pomodoro technique

Distractions are the arch-enemy of quality work: you get into the zone, and you keep being pulled out. It's like trying to deep dive with a snorkel: you have to constantly come back to the surface and start again from scratch.

That's where **time blocks** come in handy. Time blocking (also known as timeboxing) is the practice of blocking out a specific time window to work on one thing only. This works really well with themes actually, as you could have a big morning block to work on a specific theme.

The rule is to always protect your block: that's why it's important to add your most important ones to your calendar and treat them as actual meetings and commitments. It doesn't matter if you're the only participant.

Just like you would do with any other meeting, it's ok to occasionally move it to another day if another event that must happen on that time pops up (like a flight). The important thing is that this doesn't become common practice and you don't discount the commitment you have made with yourself to respect your time blocks.

Some of my favourite uses of time blocks are: writing, going through all my inboxes, planning my week, and reviewing my metrics and progress.

Time blocking fails when done too granularly: either too many blocks, bringing to a very regimented plan that cannot possibly follow the opportunities and challenges of a real day; or blocks that are too specific, giving an unrealistic amount of time to each particular task. In both cases, the plan is doomed from the start and you will end up not trusting the system and eventually abandoning it. Remember, there is no such thing as bad control: you're either in control of your day, or you're not.

A great companion for time blocking is the **pomodoro technique**. This takes its name from those tomato-shaped kitchen timers (pomodoro is italian for tomato), and it's a great way to train your focus to work on one thing at a time, so you can stick to your blocks.

The pomodoro technique alternates a 25-minute timer of deep work with a 5-minute timer of rest, allowing you to recover and always perform at your peak.

1. First, choose ONE clear task that you're going to focus on for the next 25 minutes.

2. Start the timer, and spend the next 25 minutes on that one task, without working on anything else. If you get distracted, relax – you're learning and that's ok: just acknowledge you drifted off and get back to your one task. However, if the distraction pulls you away from the task, reset the timer back to 25 minutes.

3. Once the 25 minutes are up, stop, and have a mini-celebration. You now have a 5 minute break, and it's important to respect that: switch posture, go for a brief walk, listen to a podcast, or get some water.

For most people, 25 minutes is far too long a time window to focus on one thing only. So start small: 10 minutes first, and then add 5 more once you see that you can complete the timer without getting distracted. That way you will gently train your focus and ability to concentrate.

The pomodoro technique is a great way to sprint through your time boxes, making sure you stick to your theme without getting pulled away by distractions.

The not-to-do list

The not-to-do list is the ultimate antidote to the infinite to-do list, when you keep accumulating random, unrelated tasks that keep you busy without getting you anywhere.

Your daily not-to-do list tells you explicitly what you will not be working on today, giving you permission to focus on the few things that will make a difference (and actually get them done instead of spreading yourself thin on too many things). Guilt free.

What now

This chapter was already action-packed, and I shared with you a few powerful techniques you can use to organize and own your 24 hours. Here's the recap of the action to take.

First step, liberation:

- *Look at the exercise from chapter one, and revise your long-term direction*
- *Create a list of regular activities you currently have on, and estimate how long you spend on each, every week*
- *Go through the list, and select (eliminate) activities that are not helping your long-term direction*
- *Get real, and track how you actually allocate your time. You can do this on paper, using a spreadsheet, or a time-tracking app. Make sure you do this at least once a day, using one-hour increments.*
- *Get shocked (and potentially angry at yourself).*

Now that you are aware of what activities take up your time (and how much of it), you can claim back your 24 hours by creating a plan to organise your day and week. Remember, if you don't step up and control your time, someone else will. The important thing is to record your activities and totally trust the system so you can free up headspace to focus on something else.

Here are some great techniques to take control of your time:

- *The Quick Day Planning technique*
- *Planning your week in advance*
- *Theming each day of the week*
- *Using time blocks (and the pomodoro technique)*
- *Implementing a not-to-do list*

Communication is key, especially if you are going to set restrictions and limits to the way you work, like time blocks and themes. If shared explicitly, these will actually help others know exactly when to expect you to deliver (and on what). Setting constraints without sharing expectations can leave your team confused and in the dark. Make sure that everyone on your team is on the same page, and empowered to use these powerful tools.

To make it easy, you can go through this exercise in the worksheet you downloaded at the start of the book.

You don't have to do it all at once: start small, and get more sophisticated once you get into the groove of things and have found a system that works for you.

CHAPTER EIGHT
ACCOMPLISH MORE, FASTER

"Never confuse movement with action."

Ernest Hemingway

Some of the most prestigious supercars can go from 0 to 60 mph in just over 2 seconds.

When you compare that with the average car's 8-15 seconds, the difference is big but…those 6 seconds are almost pointless for most. Even more so when you consider that the urban speed limit rarely exceeds (or even touches) 60 mph. The practical advantage is marginal, and yet, there is something fascinating about speed: the ability to defy the clock and get more done within the same span of time.

Speed is often the difference between success and failure.

Losing 5 pounds in two months would be a great result.

Losing 5 pounds in 2 years would be a disappointment.

Doubling your business in a year would be a terrific result.

Doubling it in 40 years would be a harsh failure.

Reaching another country in 2 hours means you can enjoy regular travels abroad.

Reaching another country in 2 days means you'll probably stay on the sofa instead.

Time is a massive variable in everything that we do: our minutes are limited on a daily basis, but also during our lifetime. Since we cannot trade or expand time, the ability to compress more into the same timeline is the ability to have a fuller life, filled with exponential growth and memorable events.

This book was written in just over 3 months of work between idea and final draft, with an extra 5 weeks for print and pre-launch promotion. Not only speed allowed me to leave no space to doubt and procrastinate, it also allowed me to compress more in the same timeline.

If you had to choose between writing a book in three years, or three books in one year, which would you choose?

The ability to compress the same results in less time is the ability to learn faster, compound results, and grow exponentially, all while creating intense experiences.

In 2015, I had become incredibly skinny: my health, attractiveness, and confidence were rock bottom. I had gone through a difficult time, and I wanted to change that fast so I could rebuild my whole situation. I wanted to give myself a better chance at creating a great future, and I knew that having the discipline to work on my fitness would spread to every area of my life. So I did a massive bulk up, and put on 11 pounds (5 kg) of muscle in less than 10 weeks. Though that's not the fastest bulk up ever, it was still tough: seeing that transformation allowed me to show up and see the same growth in every area of my life.

I could have done the same in a year, but I would have missed out on the compound gains in other areas and not created the momentum that changed my entire life.

Speed means achieving more, faster, but it also means enjoying the fruits of your labour earlier. Waiting is just a way to let fear get in the way and stop your momentum.

When all you have is 24 hours, managing time is a losing game, but managing the speed at which you can move through those 24 hours is key. Here's how you do it.

Focus on creation

From the "hustle" to "working hard," most of us have been taught to measure the quality of our work in terms of input: if you're not working hard (and if work doesn't feel like a chore), you're doing it wrong. This comes from generations of workers being measured and compensated in terms of hours put in, hard toil, and personal sacrifice, instead of the value created.

In the end, all that matters is your output: the quality and quantity of what you produce.

If you can achieve that effortlessly, even better: results make the process irrelevant.

When you focus on creating, you tap into the power of managing energy instead of time, like we explained in chapter four: instead of seeking "balance" and extracting value from each area of your life, you keep creating growth across all of them, and you will see how they all start to support each other.

Most people focus on doing more, faster, but what matters is to **achieve** more, faster.

In other words, it's not about being busy and starting as many things as possible, but about being effective, and finishing as many things as possible.

The impact of your 24 hours depends on what you focus on. So how can you find the right things to do?

The first step is to start with the end in mind.

The natural tendency is to just start any activity that may or may not give you results, and add as much as you can to your day: skim through an infinite number of articles, read hundreds of books just because they were recommended in podcasts, start another marketing tactic, go on yet another night at the pub with the same people.

Keep every minute busy.

In a world of unintentional busyness, the purposefully lazy wins.

Since there is only so much time in your day, doing more is a losing strategy: it waters down your efforts, keeping you from seeing any real progress.

Instead of stuffing more into your day, focus on the easiest way to get to your results.

This requires working backwards from your end goal, instead of looking forwards from your present moment. Instead of moving in any direction, you want to find the shortest line between two points: your present condition and your future result.

Instead of jumping straight into a tactic, the "how," you question the final result, the "why," and find the best way to get there.

This means focusing on the output, what you create, instead of obsessing about the input, how to stay busy. This way you can spot **high-impact activities**: those actions that will bring you disproportionate results compared to everything else.

Here are some examples.

Business

When it comes to business growth, you have many possible ways to accomplish your goals.

Say that you want to double your profits, you have many options: from starting a new marketing campaign to expanding your business, to reducing costs drastically, all the way to working with different distributors, expanding the team, doubling your prices…and so much more.

There are only so many tactics you can run at the same time, so many team members you can manage, and so many clients you can work with. To avoid overwhelm and maximise results, you must focus on what works to take you from your current level to the next one, instead of doing it all.

The same principle holds true if you want to excel in a job (or are looking for one): no matter how many tools you use there are only so many emails you can send (or job applications).

To stand above the average and gain extraordinary results in less time, you must focus on unconventional actions other people are not taking: clarify your final aim and find the best way to make it happen.

Focusing on your strengths will give you a big leg up on everyone else and add a personal touch to your interaction.

Learning

When it comes to **learning**, if you're looking to learn a new skill or get exposed to new ways of acting and thinking, there is a limited amount of books you can read, videos you can watch, and articles you can consume. Yet, there is almost an infinite supply available: according to Google, there were over 129,864,880 published books in 2009. If you read 2 books a month, it would take you over 5 million years to go through all of them. On WordPress alone (the leading blog platform), 80 million new posts are published each month. YouTube currently gets 300 hours of new video content uploaded every minute.

I like to create **learning themes** around what I am working towards: instead of just opening the next book or video that comes my way, I select some of the best ones to help me grow my skills and awareness, and accelerate my progress towards my current goals.

Social and enjoyment

When it comes to social life and enjoyment, we are spoiled for choice. From an infinite number of restaurants, bars, venues, shows, and services, it's easy to be paralysed by choice and overthink things, only to do more of the same: the same food in a slightly different restaurant, the same conversations on a slightly different day.

However, there is a limit to how many people you can have in your social life, and a limit to the number of activities you can share with others (or yourself).

That's why it's important to focus on the people that bring you growth and enjoyment, and the experiences that work for you and for the people around you. For example, though I may not see some of my closest friends as often as most people would, I focus on relationships that have a particularly high degree of affinity, and then share intense moments whenever we do meet by sharing deep experiences and conversations.

This way I can keep growing as my relationships do, instead of having to cling to them hoping they do not change.

How to find high-impact activities

The first step to find your high-impact activities is to clarify your final aim.

In certain cases, this will be measurable (like doubling your revenue), while in others it will be more conceptual (such as experiencing more joy or finding a great relationship).

For **measurable goals**, make sure you have a clear number, but also an idea of what reaching that goal would unlock. So many business owners create dull goals based on last year's performance, with no idea why that would be at all meaningful.

I worked with a client to transform the way his team worked together: after speaking to everyone individually, it was clear that the targets they had set were meaningless to them. So we made the impact clear: a new office, team breaks abroad, a new launch.

Whether you are growing a business or losing weight, make sure you internalise the impact that reaching that goal will have, or it will remain a sterile number.

For **softer goals**, take your time to explore what it means to you.

You can imagine how you will feel when the goal is reached, or go back to a time in your past when you achieved a particular state. For softer goals, self-awareness is key: you want to know what is good enough for you without having to lean on some preconception or someone else's definition.

Often, making a list of requirements is important to get clarity and direction.

For example, if your goal is to be able to take the ultimate dream vacation, then write down exactly what that looks like, point-by-point.

If you are looking to meet a great friend or an interesting date, list down the characteristics that would make them "great" or "interesting" to you.

Each descriptor will nudge your actions in the right direction and be a clear filter to select which actions to take.

The second step once you have your final aim is to make a list of possible ways to get there. As we have seen in the examples in the previous section, there are many paths to get to the same end place, so it's important you evaluate a few and not jump straight into the first one that comes to mind.

For this step, you want to decide on a target number of ideas, and then write them down in short succession. Pick a relatively high number as your aim, way above the number of ideas that come to mind immediately. Go for a minimum of 21 (I always do one extra rep).

You will find that you will struggle to get that many. The secret is not to stop: once you get past the mid-way hurdle, you will get the best ideas on how to accomplish your final goal. At this stage, don't judge your ideas as good or bad: just write them down as they come to you. Anything works.

Next, you want to select one or two actions from your list of ideas to get to your final objective. The easiest way to do this is by exclusion: pick pairs of two ideas from the list, and choose the one with the strongest potential. Cross the weakest idea off, and pair the strongest of the two with another one, until you've gone through the entire list.

Now it's time to test your idea. In order to do this, you must create a way to measure progress towards your final goal: this is usually a milestone that is closer in time to you, and represents a fraction of the ultimate target.

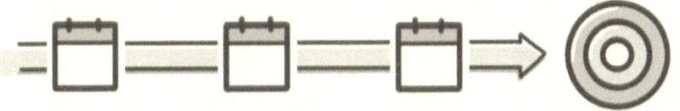

You can test whether the idea you picked will get the results that you want fast enough by comparing the results against your milestone. If it doesn't hold up, go back to your list or expand it to find new ones after learning from the previous attempt.

If you picked two ideas, you can test them against each other, compare them to the milestone, and then pick the best performing one.

Remember, in order to find a high-impact activity that will effectively get you results fast, you must:

- *Start with the end in mind and find a clear objective*
- *Ideate and collect many ways to get to your objective*
- *Divide the final objective into measurable milestones*
- *Select one or two actions, and test them against the milestone*

Ultimately, if you question measurable goals enough times, you will often get to a softer goal, based on an emotion or a sense of purpose and achievement. When it comes to these goals, knowing what will give you those results is a matter of self-awareness: being attuned to your own reactions and knowing what works for you.

Playing to your strengths

Focusing on results also means working more on your strengths than your weaknesses.

Your strengths are those activities that come easy to you and bring disproportionate results compared to those activities that you really don't want to work on. To discover your strengths, keep an eye on what comes second nature to you and what other people tend to ask you questions about (or let you work on). You can even ask your friends or your team about what your strengths are: you'll be surprised at what you take for granted about yourself!

When it comes to business or personal growth, we often get fixated on the idea of doing everything ourselves. Entrepreneurs are often guilty of this, learning basic-level skills to get something done that they don't want to do, all while taking a big chunk of time away from playing to their strengths. I have worked with founders who had taken on so much themselves that their business ended up shrinking, since they were spread too thin on activities that were "'a chore."

At home, if you have a water leak in the ceiling, you would never watch youtube videos, read books, and then start hammering to figure out how you can repair the damage yourself: you would just call an expert so you can keep working on what allows you to get results (and ultimately pay for that expert).

In chapter ten, you will learn how leveraging other people (and more) will free you up to work on your high-impact activities and shortcut your results.

Time luxuries

The first time I went on extended travels for months, it was after two years of planning and taking action towards making it happen. At that point I just needed the courage to take a leap of faith and actually go for it. Telling my story during my travels, the reaction I would get most often was, "That's really cool, I wish I could do that."

What these people missed, is that two years prior I was the person saying, "That's really cool, I wish I could do that," and that was the moment I decided to make it happen and create a system that would allow me to travel and work remotely for long periods of time.

The reason I did it is that the idea of being location independent and able to meet new people, explore new places, and be immersed in a new culture for months, is important to me. It positively impacts the quality of my time on this planet: to me, it's a **time luxury**.

We tend to think about luxury in a very material sense: an expensive handbag or a premium supercar. Time luxuries, on the other hand, are the freedom to allocate your time in ways that you value greatly and to increase the quality of your everyday.

You can buy the most expensive material luxuries, but if you are not free to experience your time in ways that bring you joy and fulfilment, you will feel time poor and material luxuries are just going to make you feel powerless and unable to truly enjoy them.

Time luxuries are not a one-off, but something you can keep as part of your lifestyle.

That's what makes them so powerful: even if it takes you a few years to get to that freedom, you will be able to enjoy that for the rest of your life.

To build this privilege, sometimes you may have to compromise on the ordinary: if you do what everyone else is doing, you will not be able to create your own time luxuries.

For example, I love being able to take a break from work at any point during the day, or to take a day off without having to justify myself. Sometimes though, that means sprinting on a particular project on a Sunday morning. Personally, I love to make every day meaningful, but the point is that in order to create extraordinary flexibility, I also had to let go of the ordinary rigidity (in this case, of the weekend).

Only you can decide which time luxuries are important to you: just as some people like watches, others like cars, and others again are into high fashion. You have to pick the time luxuries that work for you. Here are some of my favourite examples.

- *Being location independent is important to me, as it gives me the freedom to experience my time in any location, while learning new languages and creating amazing memories.*

- *Being able to sleep in when I have a late evening seeing friends (or writing the last chapter of this book).*

- *Going to the gym three to four times a week without having to be on a strict schedule: being able to go to the gym at 11am or 4pm means I can enjoy training without having to time myself around others, and I don't have to skip a workout if my plans change.*

- *Meeting friends on a casual Tuesday night instead of having to wait for the busy weekend makes my dinners much more relaxed and personal.*

- *Being able to avoid a daily commute, and being able to reach the most common places I live around is something that drastically changes the quality of my life, making me walk more, and making my social and business life much easier.*

Time luxuries impact the quality of your time, and they are different for everyone: depending on your lifestyle and personality, the ways you appreciate your time will vary.

If you're not sure what to shoot for, take a look at your inspirations: keep an eye on the people you like, the authors of the books you read, the people you follow on social media, and pick what you like from their lifestyle and how they're able to enjoy their time, and add it to your wishlist. You can then pick two or three and work on making them happen.

Now go all in

Once you find ways that give you a lot of results per minute, be ruthless and eliminate what doesn't work as well, so you can free up time to do more high-impact activities.

Remember: saying no to things that don't meet the same standard is how you'll get to say yes to more of what works.

So go all in on what brings you disproportionate results:

The relationships that bring you the most joy; the tactics that bring you more business growth; the activities that make you feel refreshed and recharged.

High-impact activities can be applied to any area of your life, and finding what really works can save you weeks, months, or even years of useless effort, all while shortcutting your results. To find them, use the step-by-step above, and remember the yes/no rule: experiment broadly first, commit to what works, and say no to everything else.

That's how you can compress more in the same time: by focusing on results, not effort.

What now

It's time to find your own high-impact activities.

These will allow you to get results faster and compress more activities into your time: remember that what matters is output (results) rather than input (effort).

The first step is to find your main goal: whether it's a measurable or soft target, by questioning it and asking "why," you can get to the core goal. Make sure you break it down into milestones, so you can measure your progress (and adjust course before it's too late).

The second step is to identify your personal strengths.

What comes natural to you? Focus on those activities that have brought you results in the past or that other people value or are not able to carry out. When in doubt, ask them.

The third step is to spot your high-impact activities:

- *Start with the end in mind and find a clear objective*
- *Ideate and collect many ways to get to your objective*
- *Divide the final objective into measurable milestones*
- *Select one or two actions and test them against the milestone*

Now that you have your high-impact activities, you are ready to see disproportionate results.

All it takes is to start taking action.

CHAPTER NINE
MULTIPLY THE VALUE OF YOUR TIME

"A man who dares to waste one hour of time has not discovered the value of life."

Charles Darwin

If time had a fixed value, increasing your wealth would require you to increase the amount of time you work proportionally. If that was the case, someone in a 9-5 job earning $50,000 a year would have to work an impossible 80 hours a day in order to earn $500,000.

Clearly, there must be some value beyond the clock.

Why can some people charge $5,000 for a single call, while others are paid below $8 an hour? Why can some people generate money while sleeping, while others can't take a single day off?

By now, you should know the secret: time is worthless.

It's what you choose to do during that time that creates any value.

The one hour I spent queuing up at a post office in Portugal (only to find out I'd have to come back the next day) isn't even comparable to an hour serving a coaching client, sharing a meaningful experience with a friend, closing a business deal, or talking at an event full of entrepreneurs.

The same amount of time can evoke positive emotions or none at all, change the course of your life or have no impact, teach you a lesson or nothing new, generate more resources or leave you empty. That's why increasing the value of your time is fundamental for yourself, your business, your relationships, and anything you want to accomplish in life.

It will also give you an unfair advantage: everyone has the same 24 hours. If you're just trading time, competition is fierce – anyone can sell their 24 hours for a lower price.

Time is a commodity: everyone has the same amount. When all you do is sell hours, it becomes a race to the bottom. But when you increase the value of your time, that's when you can live an extraordinary life, create memorable moments, and generate value for others to get paid what you deserve.

To increase the value of your own 24 hours, you must first understand and internalise three rules, which may go against how most people see time.

Rule #1: time is limited and available in equal quantities to everyone

We all have the same cap: 24 hours a day. No one gets 10 hours a day, and no one gets 97. **Twenty-four is the number.** When you behave like time is infinite, it's easy to get lost doing too many things that get you nowhere.

In business: getting lost in 2000 tactics (or products), looking for the next shortcut that will do the work for you.

In life: saying yes to friends that drain you, to choices that take you nowhere, to activities and empty promises you feel half-hearted about.

That's the attitude of those who think time is infinite, and one choice will not preclude another. Instead, focus on mastering your few strengths and fostering those activities and people that bring you disproportionate returns: achievement, joy, growth, so you can squeeze as much as you can out of your 24 hours.

Rule #2: time has no intrinsic value

Most people behave like time has value per se, but let's think about this one. An hour reading emails and blogs may make me feel busy, but it's the one hour spent calling a warm lead that is going to grow my business. Same time, different value.

An hour scrolling through Instagram may make me feel like I have people in my life, but it's the one hour sharing a real experience that's going to grow lifelong friendships. Same time, different value.

Thinking that time has some sort of value is what's keeping you busy, working on what doesn't move the needle. It's the idea that time is worth something that keeps you glued to the wrong things for hours and hours, without questioning what you are actually spending time on. **Your time is worthless.**

Spending two hours at the gym checking your phone on the Stairmaster is going to give you zero results compared to an intense 20m workout.

Watching yet another Netflix show before bed is not going to add any value to your life compared to watching your favourite film with a friend.

One hour having the same conversations with the same people at the same bar isn't going to grow your friendships like creating a memorable experience within the same one hour.

A day reading random blogs won't give you nearly as much as learning and applying specific information from a single source.

Notice how it's often a case of intentionality, not what activity you choose.

Reading, video games, the gym, can all sit anywhere on the spectrum from "wasting time" to "investing time" according to how much you put in and…how much you'll get out of it.

It's not enough to show up: you need to choose the right activities and be intentional.

The more you put into it, the more you will get out of it.

Rule #3 – the only time that matters is now

Behaving like time is infinite makes you put off those things that you actually care about.

Thinking that you'll get another chance tomorrow, and the day after, and again, makes you put off taking action and doing what actually matters to you.

No one decides to be stuck in a business that sucks all their free time. Or a job that takes away their energy. Or a relationship that is just "ok."

Waiting for the future is what keeps you stuck, deciding not to take action in the present. Whether it's your daily 24 hours, or the average lifespan of 40 million minutes, our time isn't infinite. And it happens now.

Increase the value of time, today

Now we know: focusing on quantity is a losing strategy – we all get the same amount of time.

The key to increasing the value of your time is to focus on high-impact activities that bring you results. Instead of trying to do everything, you choose what works.

Step #1: elimination

The first step to increasing the value of your time is saying no.

This book has a whole chapter (chapter three) on the power of saying no – to be able to focus on the few choices that bring you results, you must say no to the many that get you nowhere.

Again, it's the trade-off of only having 24 hours.

To make space for life-changing activities, you must say no to those activities that are worthless, bring you no pleasure, give you no growth, generate zero value.

The more noes you'll be able to say, the more the worth of your time will increase, because you will be able to focus on what actually generates more value for yourself and others with every moment. To increase the quality of your relationships, you must say no to what doesn't meet the standard. To increase your business rate, you must say no to clients that cannot meet the requirement. If you don't let go, you will stay anchored to what you actually want to change.

When you focus on your core strengths most of the time, and then use the principle of leverage to use other people's, that's when you can see disproportionate results.

In the last chapter, we looked at how you can find and focus on high-impact activities only, and use other people's to do the rest (as you will see in the next chapter).

When you are not comfortable letting go and delegating, you spread yourself thin on "everything" and end up losing track of what got you where you are.

Remember to focus on output, not input; quality, not quantity.

Step #2: invest in yourself

Learning is one of the best ways to increase your value, and consequently the value of your time. This spans from self-awareness to new skills that unlock something else that you want.

Learning and practicing new skills not only makes you more effective, it also makes you more valuable to other people, and therefore able to generate more income per hour.

When you focus on high-value skills (like programming, copywriting, sales, communication…) you will gain timeless ways to move beyond selling your minutes: you will be able to sell the value created with your time.

When it comes to learning, you are already ahead of the game: the average American reads four books a year or less. By picking this book up, you are investing in yourself and increasing the value of your time by mastering the game of squeezing more out of your day.

Instead of playing the quantity game like everyone else, you are generating output.

Without realising it, you already have some high-value skills that you take for granted. For example, if you're reading this page it's likely you can speak English, and teach others. We tend to take our strengths for granted because they are second-nature to us.

Whatever your high-value skill, by investing in yourself you are shifting your attention from selling time to creating value, and that's what matters.

Whether it's for financial gains or personal fulfilment, you want to get as much as possible out of every minute. By investing in yourself, learning new skills, and gaining more self-awareness, you can get disproportionate results out of the same time everyone else has too.

Step #3: make time valuable

If time is money, how can you increase the monetary value of your time?

The first step is to charge based on value rather than based on time. Most people are paid for a certain amount of hours (like the 9-5), which is actually a punishing system: the time required and the compensation given will remain the same, irrespective of your results. Therefore, it incentivizes striving for the minimum level of action that will not get you fired or replaced.

Even if you're a contractor charging per hour (or per day), you will eventually run into trouble: though you can sometimes claim back variables like time spent and location, many clients will try to work out your day rate from an employed system, purely because that's their reference point when it comes to hourly compensation. This creates a major cap, and sometimes sparks unnecessary misunderstandings between client and contractor.

The issue is that you're still charging based on something that has no fixed value: time.

When you move to setting your prices based on value, that's when you remove the cap from how much you can earn from your work. This also incentivizes you to do only remarkable work, since the market will reward or punish you according to what you are able to deliver (rather than by your time passing). The value you create depends on your work as much as it does on the kind of clients you work with, as that will determine the scale of your impact.

For example, let's say you can create a new e-commerce website that performs 10% better: a $1,000/mo store may be losing money on the change, while a $100k/mo store would probably be able to absorb that cost in a heartbeat.

In other words, when you charge based on the value you create, there is no limit to how much you can charge, as long as you select who to work with to maximise your impact.

Charging based on value is fair on all parties, because it can only work when real value is created: if you don't deliver, the market will knock you down one rung, and someone else will take over.

Step #4: make time irrelevant

When it comes to the monetary value of time, the final step is to reduce the link between time and value. This can be done by creating products or productising your services.

Products scale infinitely beyond your time: whether it's a digital or a physical product, how many you sell each day isn't limited by your time.

Productising services means creating standard packages that you can then train someone else to offer on your behalf. This way, you can focus on growing the brand and finding more work to send to your team.

Somehow, the online myth is that creating a successful product is easy. This is not what I'm trying to communicate in this book: products aren't the panacea of your problems, but they are the ultimate way to disengage time from value, and scale way beyond your 24 hours.

Here's a story that explains why products are great: some time ago, I invited a girl I was seeing to a concert. The next morning, I walked to my living room and opened my laptop to book tickets. As I checked my inbox, I had a notification saying that someone had joined one of my online courses (while I was sleeping), essentially paying for my concert tickets. I thought, "Thank you man from America!" and felt amazing to have a system that worked while I didn't.

If you like this story, here's a challenge to you: find something around the house you don't need, and sell it on eBay. Though you will have to figure out a lot of logistics (like shipping), it will show you that you can make money through a product, and create momentum towards working on a product of your own one day.

These principles apply beyond money: even in your personal life, you want to focus on what brings you the most results so you can squeeze as much value as possible.

What brings you the most joy?

What gives you exponential growth?

Which people make you feel recharged the most?

Which activities and places give you the most pleasure?

Know what works for you and do more of it, instead of going for quantity on things that give you limited results. This applies to every choice and area of life.

This is known as the Pareto principle, or the 80/20 approach: the majority of results (output) will come from a minority of actions (input).

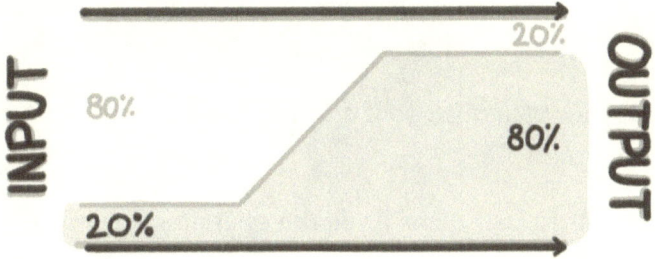

Though the ratio isn't always fixed to 80/20, knowing that this principle exists will empower you to look for what really works (and do more of it), and abandon those things that give you only marginal gains. That way you can optimise your actions to get better results.

Just like you learned in chapter three, saying no to anything that doesn't bring any significant impact is key to being able to do more of what actually matters.

Here's a quick exercise you can use to understand what's worth your time, and select activities that increase the value you can generate with your 24 hours.

Calculate your dream rate

I was writing this very book, and it was time to take a break: I'm a big fan of butter coffee, and I was looking forward to making a boosting decaf in between pages. When I opened the fridge however, I was out of butter. Oh no. I put my coat on, ready to go and fetch some of my favourite. Until I realised that it was going to take me nearly an hour and the results wouldn't have matched my dream rate. Not even close. I immediately took my coat off and kept writing.

Here's how to calculate your dream rate and use it to filter your activities.

This is particularly useful if you run a business, but even if you are employed at someone else's company, you can use it to select the activities that will take you to the next level.

First, you must establish your next monetary goal: how much do you or your business want to earn in the next year? This should be based on your current situation, but it's better to overshoot than to go for small increments. Let's pick $100,000.

Now, you must decide the terms of your work. How many days a year do you want to take completely off? How many hours do you want to work? Let's call it 65 days totally off (300 days on), and an average 5 hours of work per day. That leaves us with 5 x 300 = 1,500 hours a year.

All you have to do to figure out your dream rate, is to divide your annual results by the amount of hours you want to work. In our example, that's $67 an hour.

Notice how that makes it a lot more realistic. Especially thinking about all the possibilities we discussed in this chapter to increase the value of your time.

Whatever your dream rate is, you can now use it as a filter for anything that you do.

For example, ordering groceries online could save you many hours a week, all for a few dollars. In the meantime, you can use that time for something you either truly enjoy or that generates more than your dream rate.

The point is to change your behaviour so that it supports your results, instead of waiting to do it the other way around. Now you have a clear way to measure the value of your time.

When working, focus on what generates your dream rate or above; when enjoying your time, focus on activities that you value at more than your dream rate.

What now

In this chapter, we went through the three fundamental rules that govern the value of your time, and went through many ways to increase the value of your time.

From eliminating what doesn't work to investing in yourself, all the way to increasing the monetary value of time, make sure you review the actions in this chapter that resonated with you and implement them in your life. Information on its own will make you very knowledgeable, but it's only paired with action that information becomes transformation.

Lastly, work out your dream rate, and use it to filter out all your activities so that you can maximise your enjoyment and effectiveness. This simple tool will help you match your actions to your goals.

CHAPTER TEN
LEVERAGE: EXPAND BEYOND YOURSELF

*"Alone we can do so little;
together we can do so much."*

Helen Keller

Life is a social activity. If you have a business, you need people to sell to you, buy from you, and work with you. If you have a job, you need someone to give you tasks, pay your salary, and possibly work together in a team. If you want to learn a skill, having someone else inspire you and then teach you their knowledge is the best shortcut. If you want to create something truly impactful, you need others to help. If you want to create amazing experiences, you need others to share them with (and provide the services to make them possible). Heck, even if you want to spend me-time watching Netflix, you need other people to leave you alone.

Relationships are one of the main ingredients of human life.

Our dreams, challenges, and motivation all come from the people we surround ourselves with. We are shaped by the people we keep around: by their actions and their standards. Whether it's through a YouTube video, a book, a conversation with a friend, or seeing your parents do something, the people you associate and identify with shape your expectations you have of yourself.

Whenever I travel for extended periods of time, I always look for outdoor training spots where other people workout from regularly. I could work out from home, but that wouldn't put me in front of people regularly looking after their bodies and performance. I wouldn't have anyone to push my performance or inspire me. By training around other high-performance people I am pushed to keep my training up and even do better. It reminds me that growth never ends.

Shortcutting your results

When you take on too much, you will always feel like you never have enough time.

Even if we assume that you are the best person at everything (and let's be honest, that's never the case), you cannot do it all. You will run out of time way too early.

Yet we often insist on doing everything ourselves: getting in shape without any guidance, taking on a new challenge without the support of our group, even starting a business project without having any customers.

Insisting on doing everything yourself is a buffer to protect you against perceived risk. The risk of getting rejected by your customers, of depending on other people, of not being able to back out of a commitment, of leading others, of being found out for not being good enough.

So we go it alone, taking on as much as we can until we run into the 24-hour cap and get stuck, not able to take any more on, and only seeing results after a long time (if we don't give up in the meantime).

When you do everything yourself, it's impossible to know what you don't know.

You are constantly trying to guess what will work, stumbling forward without knowing where each action will take you.

Your resources are naturally capped: you can make more money, you can make more friends, you can find a new job or more customers, but you cannot generate more than 24 hours a day.

You literally don't have time to do everything yourself.

That's where leverage comes into place. By using other people's resources, you can move beyond your 24-hour cap. In the words of Archimedes, "Give me a lever long enough and a fulcrum on which to place it and I will move the world." That's because leverage allows you to multiply your efforts and move something really big with minimum effort. In the rest of this chapter, I want to show you five ways you can use leverage to multiply your time.

Leverage time

The first way is to leverage other people's time.

This is when you delegate work that you shouldn't be doing yourself to other people, so you can focus on your strengths. You can look at chapter three to establish what you should and shouldn't be doing, so you can increase the value of your time.

As a quick recap, you should select anything that doesn't leverage your own strengths, anything that isn't aligned with your desired hourly rate, and anything that isn't a significant priority. You can use someone else's time to essentially buy yourself more time, and assign your own 24 hours to what matters.

Here are some easy examples of time leverage.

Use drivers and taxis. When I started getting taxis from the airport to the city centre whenever I was traveling, it felt a bit wrong. Until I realised that I could work during the ride or get to my next appointment more quickly. The ride saved me time, and all I had to do was focus on activities that generated more than the fee. Remember, you can create more money per minute, but you cannot create more time per minute.

Get a cleaner. This is an easy one: it will make you more efficient, and save you hours doing something most people do not enjoy. All you have to do to justify this is to focus on high-impact activities.

Work with employees, collaborators, and contractors. Instead of learning everything yourself (and doing a mediocre job), collaborate with other people that can generate results for you by leveraging their own strengths and freeing up time for you to use yours.

By working with other people, you can focus on the vision and direction instead of being stuck "in" the business all the time.

Work with a Virtual Assistant. From handling your calendar to getting your intel prepped before a meeting, a VA can take a lot of petty tasks off your plate, which add up to many hours a week.

I started having a VA in my first full-time job, and it was great to take care of small personal tasks so I could make the most of my limited time outside the office. At a recent event, I even met someone who had outsourced their IT job to someone in Bangalore: though eventually they got caught and fired, it shows how much leveraging others can do for you.

Leverage knowledge

The second way is to leverage other people's skills and knowledge.

You don't have enough time to learn everything yourself, especially by direct experience.

To be clear: experience is the best teacher. Make mistakes, adjust, learn what works. But because we only have 24 hours a day, there's only so much we can learn ourselves. Plus, I don't want to learn everything. There are skills that I will never master and I never should, so I can focus on sharpening my existing talents.

For example, I have no interest in mastering law (and it doesn't even sound like a good idea), and would rather use my own strengths to generate the resources to use someone else's knowledge and experience in the field.

Here are some of the ways you can leverage skills and knowledge.

Tap into other people's knowledge by taking courses and reading books: a great way to use someone else's lessons and mistakes to progress in your own journey.

This can save you months and years, as well as open you up to possibilities you might have never known existed otherwise. It's important to combine this with action, though, or knowledge alone can be used as a way to procrastinate what's scary.

A more direct way to tap into other people's knowledge is to work with a coach.

For example, I work with top-performing entrepreneurs worldwide committed to growing their business and creating an uncompromising lifestyle. By working with me, they tap into my own knowledge as well as the experience of all my past and present clients. You wouldn't be able to scale that.

Coaches, trainers, and mentors are a great way to directly leverage knowledge while also baking in the power of accountability and commitment. Only by using leverage can you get that much experience.

You can also combine leveraging knowledge and time by hiring a specialist that can take care of a specific task for you. An example could be hiring a lawyer, an accountant, a great sales copy writer: someone that helps you optimise your work while you focus on doing your magic.

Leverage money

The third way to go beyond your 24 hours is to leverage other people's money.

Often, we let money get in the way of our potential actions: we have a plan, but we may not have the cash flow to execute it at scale. So we wait until we have the resources, and in the meantime waste the only one that cannot be renewed or multiplied: time.

By leveraging other people's monetary resources, you can shortcut growth by providing value both ways. Here are a few examples.

Crowdfunding platforms allow anyone with an idea to validate it, and then even get sales and cash upfront before having to manufacture anything.

Kickstarter alone helped thousands of projects raise billions of dollars in total, turning many ideas from a few thousand dollars of budget to 6 or 7 figures. Granted, such a jump requires a lot of work, but by leveraging other people's money (and validating the product) you shortcut growth and reach results faster.

A loan towards getting an asset, such as a cash flow positive business or a flat that can be rented out (or airbnb'd) to cover the entire monthly payment, is another way to leverage someone else's money. The asset will then pay for the loan, as well as generate a surplus of money, without having to wait for the resources upfront.

Looking for investment in your business or project is another way to leverage other people's money (often, as well as leveraging their knowledge): though this dilutes the percentage you own, it can potentially grow the overall pie for everyone, making your slice worth more and enabling you to finally reach the next level in your project.

Leverage allows you to multiply the power of your own money and to generate greater results faster. As we have seen, debt is only one of many ways to leverage other people's money, but it's important to distinguish leverage from bad debt: using other people's money (like a credit card or a loan) to buy clothes, a holiday you can't afford, or even a house is not leveraging money. By now, this should sound like taking on time debt, putting the responsibility of your current results on your future self.

Leverage relationships

The fourth way is to leverage other people's relationships.

You can meet as many people as you like in life, but we are naturally capped to how many relationships we can maintain. Not only do we have limited time daily (the 24-hour cap), our social cognitive capacity is limited too. This is estimated to be around 150 social connections at any one time, known as Dunbar's number[14].

Instead of starting from scratch, sieving through a plethora of people you might meet, and then leaning on your network alone, you can leverage other people's relationships to meet incredible friends, generate business deals, find an exciting new job, and more.

Here are some of my favourite ways to leverage other people's relationships:

---

[14] R.I.M.Dunbar, 'Neocortex size as a constraint on group size in primates', *Journal of Human Evolution*, vol 22, 69 (1992), pp. 469-493.

Organise dinners for other people: I love to organise dinner for strangers once a quarter, in which I bring together 6 people that don't know each other but should. By asking my co-host to bring someone I don't know (but should meet) and doing the same for them, we create a great evening of amazing conversations amongst like-minded people.

The nature of the conversation and the event itself help us shortcut creating a relationship into just a few hours.

Ask for an introduction every time you meet someone new. This was a game-changer for me: I meet a lot of people both on and offline, by reaching out directly, receiving requests, and asking for introductions.

Every time I have a chat with someone new, I ask them to introduce me to someone I should meet (and do the same for them)—a total multiplier!

Releasing interviews and creating amazing content for others will get you in front of their audience, whether it's an event, a podcast, a blog, or a video channel.

This is a way to leverage quantity of relationships, and going broad instead of deep.

Ask for matchmaking: asking for introductions is a great way to meet the exact people you're looking for. The secret is to be very specific as to what you're after in order to make the matchmaker's job as easy and smooth as possible.

You can ask past clients for great referrals, you can ask friends to meet new friends, or even ask for help finding a great business partner.

Joint ventures: a great way to accelerate business growth is to work with other people and sell products together. This can be a collaboration on a new product or launch, or it can be an affiliate deal in which one party gets a percentage cut for every sale or referral they generate for the other party.

The best thing about leveraging relationships is the win-win-win multiplier effect: everyone wins by expanding their network and by providing value to the important people in it.

Leverage technology

The fifth and last way to leverage resources beyond your 24 hours is to use technology.

Using technology means using software and hardware to automate as many tasks as possible and to become very efficient at those you want to do yourself.

This doesn't mean downloading 2,000 apps on your phone: optimising things that you should not do, or perfecting them to a level that only brings you small, incremental results is busy procrastination.

You can leverage technology to be faster at communication, more efficient, and to have access to more opportunities.

For example, once I outlined this book, I recorded my voice to create a first transcript using my phone and a quick transcription service, and then turned the transcripts into a final draft. Another way I love to use technology is the software that allows me to keep in touch with my connections, and to keep connected to my blog readers and email list, as well as creating content on the go.

What now

The five ways to leverage your 24 hours and go beyond your limited resources are leveraging other people's time, other people's skills and knowledge, other people's money, other people's relationships, and technology.

Remember, your actions are capped to how much work you can fit into your 24 hours: use leverage to expand beyond it.

Here's the action for this chapter: look at the list of activities you created in chapter one, then look at your main goal for the moment, and write down three ways you can use leverage to multiply your impact and speed.

Don't just say "leverage time." Whose time? What can you outsource? For each step, be very specific and then actually take action, so you can see your workload drop and your results skyrocket.

CHAPTER ELEVEN
BACK TO THE FUTURE

"Think of yourself as dead. You have lived your life. Now, take what's left and live it properly."

Marcus Aurelius

Every few months, I host this strange dinner combining people that don't know each other, and ask them each to bring a question. One question particularly stuck with me:

"If you had one year left to live, what would you do differently?"

The idea is that, faced with limited time, we would finally change those aspects of our life that don't satisfy us: start a new adventure, spend more time with our family and friends, stop draining activities and let go of poisonous thoughts and relationships. After all, we have all read a story of how people turn their behaviour around when diagnosed with an illness, to focus on what truly matters to them and beyond them.

The point is, we don't have to use our imagination: our time is finite.

Having possible decades ahead of us instead of a single year should actually be a reason to make that change happen faster, so you can let go of the negatives as quickly as possible and enjoy the positives as long as you can. Yet, in a weird way, we weigh decades of compromises as more bearable and let things move along unchanged.

In the Middle Ages, the concept of "memento mori" was popularised, a Latin phrase meaning "remember that you have to die." This wasn't about being sad about the finite nature of our life experience, but rather being appreciative for the days we are given.

Instead of taking them for granted, celebrate them by living fully instead of postponing the important to a better time. You could say it's an exercise in gratitude, where you focus on something you tend to take for granted, like the present day, and decide to make the most of it instead of waiting for a better one which may or may not exist.

When we think of life as infinite, we discount the present, postponing what matters until later on. In the end, lost in the unimportant, we never actually do it.

As humans, we have an incredible superpower: the power of **imagination**.

We can imagine things that don't even exist yet, like an idea or a product that has never been created before. We can envision a trip that we haven't yet made, see every detail and even organise it in advance. We can imagine goals and activities we want to accomplish, and see them with precision before they even get close.

We can trigger a different emotional state by tapping into a memory or even a thought, and completely disassociate ourselves from the present situation.

You may be on a train full of exhausted people, and in your mind be scheming your next trip abroad, triggering a big smile on your face in spite of what's around you.

Most of the time though, we let our imagination work against us.

This superpower has the potential to help us create a new reality, but it can also keep us stuck in place for a very long time.

The majority of us spend the day time travelling, never truly present, constantly held back by the scar of a negative moment in the past, or the fear of a possible setback in the future.

In the meantime, we miss every present opportunity to make things different, constantly thinking about what didn't work out and what could go wrong: I could have, I should have, I would have. This creates a paralysing anxiety, spreading us thin thinking about the infinite imaginary problems in our possible futures and taking our energy away from what's happening right in front of us: the present moment.

Instead of facing the day and creating something great, we look ahead and try to avoid what could go wrong: we play not to lose instead of playing to win.

Worse still, we are wired to spot negative things: the brain is constantly scanning the environment around us, looking for potential danger.

Technically, this happens in the Reticular Activating System, the filter that decides what information gets passed from the nervous system to the brain. Potential dangers and recurrent thoughts are usually what gets through.

Negativity has priority access to our attention.

Research[15] has shown that negative emotions narrow the mind, focusing our thoughts on the problem.

When we're being chased by a sabertooth tiger, that's very useful. The mind is one-pointed towards running for our lives. Staying alive is the main and only objective.

But when we're chased by daily fears, recurring thoughts, or gloomy headlines about the possible and imaginary outcomes

---

[15] Fredrickson B.L., Joiner T., *'Positive emotions trigger upward spirals toward emotional well-being'*, 2002, in US National Library of Medicine (University of Michigan)

of the latest political drama, running for our lives won't help. And staying alive isn't a good enough daily objective.

This creates a vicious circle, where negativity breeds more negativity, the mind can only think about the problem, and

thoughts become so focused that we stop noticing the positives all around us.

There's a better way to time travel using our imagination: we can move to the future, while also appreciating what we have right now. When we're grounded in the present, we can use our imagination to shape the future and direct our lives: instead of a random succession of choices, challenges, and adventures, our actions become aligned.

When we do that, we can tap into the power of investing time and compounding actions.

That is only possible by appreciating our starting point, and the only time we can action: this very moment. Now.

A good friend of mine spent three years in the Israeli Army special forces: when he joined, he went through months of tough physical and mental training. One of the lessons that stuck with him for life is one on orienteering: how to find your way when you're lost. If you are lost and on your own, you should use your compass to go back to the last place where you had your bearing, and then figure out the rest from there.

The idea is that, when faced with a state of total confusion, you should go back to the last place where you didn't feel confused: once you have one reference point, everything else seems to make sense in relation to it.

Find your North Star, and your compass suddenly will make sense.

Wherever you are right now, you cannot create a better future unless you are grounded in the present. If you keep battling the past, or fearing tomorrow, you don't have a point of reference to start moving in a different direction.

Make long term decisions

In four research studies[16], participants interacted with realistic computer renderings of their older selves using immersive virtual reality hardware: in all cases, those who interacted with

---

[16] Hershfield, H. E., Goldstein, D. G., Sharpe, W. F., Fox, J., Yeykelis, L., Carstensen, L. L., & Bailenson, J. N. (2011). INCREASING SAVING BEHAVIOR THROUGH AGE-PROGRESSED RENDERINGS OF THE FUTURE SELF. JMR, *Journal of marketing research*, 48, S23–S37. doi:10.1509/jmkr.48.SPL.S23

their virtual future selves exhibited an increased tendency to accept later rewards over immediate ones. They started thinking longer term.

There's a great way to use your imaginative superpower to **enjoy the present** while also thinking more broadly to **positively influence the future.** To make things happen right now, while working towards a constantly better situation. Sounds too good to be true?

The secret is to forget about yourself. You don't exist.

No, I don't mean you have to ground yourself, avoid everyone else and "hustle." By now you now the secret: feeling busy doing unnecessary work till the small hours of the morning is just another way to procrastinate on the important and feel like the world would stop without your hard work (it won't).

Instead of waiting for a better future or staying stuck in instant gratification, you can both enjoy the present and create growth in the future, just by using what I call the You+10 rule.

Here's how it works. Instead of having to constantly choose between present enjoyment and future growth, you focus on decisions that will benefit your 10-year-older self. This is a simple way to measure the magnitude of your actions and choose the one that are most impactful in both the present and the future.

In 2018, I put myself on a 3 month travel ban. The rules were: no overnight friends visits, and no overnight trips outside the city of Manchester, where I lived.

I had to say no to friends visiting from London and Warsaw, while at the same time turn down travel invitations from friends. Yet, having 3 months of uninterrupted focus allowed me to restructure my business and travel for over 200 days throughout the rest of the year, living in 6 cities across 6 different countries.

This was an experience I will never forget, creating incredible memories with friends as well as on my own, and growing my standard expectations to include long-term travels.

While a weekend break would have been nice (but easily forgettable), my first extended travels changed my life and transformed my thinking: they created extraordinary present experience, and long-lasting ripples and memories way beyond the next decade.

This applies to the small things too, like the activities you choose, the projects you embark on, or even the food you eat. For example, I'm pretty particular when it comes to what I eat: I know that my nutrition will determine the quality of my life and my performance, in the present and the future.

Not surprisingly, I have a system to decide what to eat and what not to eat daily, based on research and personal experiments including blood tests and measuring my nervous system activity. This system has served me well and will continue to do so.

When I do eat out though, I make sure it's special: if I travel, I ask locals for the best places in town, and I go all in. I will never forget a world-class crab ceviche I had in Greece while looking at the sun setting beyond the sea waves.

If I'm with friends, I create adventures and experiences instead of forgettable catch ups over the same cocktails, or watching a numbing TV show together. From visiting a monastery hidden in the mountains to firing guns at the shooting range in Eastern Europe, shared moments grow friendships stronger and create unforgettable experiences: ten years from now, we'll still be talking about them.

Creating memorable experiences doesn't need to be expensive, either. Exploring a local park, bringing together strangers for dinner, and interviewing each other in a coffee shop, are all great ways to create lifelong experiences that grow relationships that are here to stay.

This is the real impact of thinking long-term: not a way to negate the present, but a way to intentionally celebrate it, all while creating the space to focus on long-lasting change and ambitious plans.

This simple rule can be applied to everything in life, in order to maximise the impact in the present and in the future. 10 years from now…

Will I remember this?

What will the impact of this be?

Would I still want to be doing this?

These simple questions can help you gauge the present and future impact of your experiences, relationships, business moves, career, travels, and even skills you want to learn. Anything can be filtered through the You+10 rule to maximise the impact.

If it's not something that will have an impact 10 years from now, then it's likely that the present impact is marginal too.

Remember, with 24 hours a day, we cannot manage time, but we can manage our choices: we cannot do everything, but we can focus on what creates the greatest, longest lasting impact.

That's how you create the future without sacrificing the present. And vice versa.

Forget incremental goals

I kept wishing for things to be different, and they never were: I wanted more friends, more clients, more fun, more fitness. I was rebuilding my life, and it wasn't happening.

Until one day, I took a piece of paper and wrote down 8 things I wanted to make happen within 3 years.

At the time, I really wanted change to happen fast, so thinking so far ahead was a mental stretch: I didn't want to wait three years for things to shift. The only thing I knew was that what I was currently doing was not working for me. I kept thinking short term, and all I was doing was digging myself in a deeper hole.

That piece of paper allowed me to let my imagination free and really focus on what was important to me. After that day, change happened almost immediately: I put on 5kg of muscle in 10 weeks, met amazing people, and started a business that would change my life forever. Without that list, this book would never exist.

Here's the truth: when you want things to change right away, all you can think of is tiny incremental change, and it never happens.

Here's why:

When you focus on short term goals, you are shackled by your present limitations: the resources available to you, your present skills, contacts, and needs.

But when you give yourself the space to think ahead, suddenly all of those limits fall off.

At the end of chapter one, we went through a quick exercise: thinking back 5 years from now to see what life was like. It's likely that your situation, your outlook on life, and your personality were very different then. Whether you want it or not, change happens fast.

When you give yourself the space to think ahead, suddenly you have no reference point: you will be a different person, with different skills, connections, and ambitions. It's impossible for you to know now, and that gives you the opportunity to paint your most ambitious plans on a blank canvas. Instead of going for small, incremental change, you can shoot for exponential growth: when you do that, the level of action you have to take will bring results very quickly.

Secondly, any significant change takes time. Short term thinking gives you the illusion that you can switch your course in a heartbeat, and in the meantime you're stuck on the same path.

Thinking longer term and using the You+10 rule gives you the runway for real, significant change to happen. And results will show up fast as you course correct.

Lastly, wanting results short term focuses you on what you want to have rather than what you want to create. Here's the problem with that: in order to change your results, you must change your actions. To change your actions, you must change your identity.

You have likely come across Albert Einstein's quote saying that "the definition of insanity is doing the same thing over and over and expecting different results."

Giving yourself the space to think longer term allows you to question your actions, try different approaches, learn new skills, and ultimately transform your results. This takes time though: the same actions that got you here will produce the same results that you are currently experiencing.

The best way to change the way you think and act is to shift your identity: if you change who you are, your expectations will change. For example, if you think of yourself as an athlete, training regularly will slowly become second nature rather than something you have to force yourself to do. If you identify as an entrepreneur, you will start to love solving problems for others and will have to find a way to do so.

However, shifting your identity takes time: you cannot change who you are and how you see yourself overnight. When you start thinking longer term, that's when you can change who you are, how you act, and ultimately the results you are getting.

Instead of looking for shortcuts all the time, give yourself the space to set huge goals, enjoy the process, and watch the magic unfold: **the long way is the shortcut.**

What now

In this chapter, you learned how thinking long term is the best way to enjoy the short term.

Here's my challenge to you: look back on the exercise from chapter one, where you wrote about a day in the life of your future self.

Now go through your current activities, choices, and relationships, and separate the ones that will be part of that future from the ones that won't. You probably have guessed the next step: go all in on the former, and make sure to add more of them so you can foster that future.

Then, use the You+10 rule to maximise your present enjoyment while boosting your future growth. Here are some great questions you can use to filter your decisions and upgrade the experiences and actions in you life:

- *Will I remember this 10 years from now?*
- *What impact will this have 10 years from now?*
- *Would I still want to be doing this 10 years from now?*

Using the principles and tools you have learned in this book, you will be able to maximise your present enjoyment, all while skyrocketing your results in the short term AND the long term. By investing your time, you will be able to see positive change and compound growth, so you can keep stacking extraordinary results, memories, relationships, and ultimately increase the value of your time.

That's how to be time rich.

CHAPTER TWELVE
WHAT NOW

"A path is made by walking on it."

Chuang Tzu

Thank you for reading this book. I appreciate the time you dedicated to reading these pages with me.

You're on your way to outperforming most of the population: though most CEOs and high-performers read multiple books a month, most Americans read under 4 books a year[17].

You are in the minority, and that's a good thing. But with privileges also come responsibilities: if some concepts resonated with you from the book, now you have no excuse not to take action. It's up to you to turn information into transformation, for yourself and for other people around you.

---

[17] Andrew Perrin, *Slightly fewer Americans are reading print books, new survey finds*, 2015

Let me know one thing you will do differently, and share a picture of you with this book: you can find me on social at @mattsandrini, or send me an email at timezillionaire.com

Don't forget to **download your workbook** to take action and apply the concepts in this book to your daily life by going to

timezillionaire.com/invest-bonus

One last thing before you go: once you're done, please give this book to a friend. Or buy them a copy. As you know by now, leveraging your connections will make it so much easier for you to take control of your time and see disproportionate results in life and business.

I'm excited about your journey.

Your friend,

Matt Sandrini

www.ingramcontent.com/pod-product-compliance
Lightning Source LLC
Chambersburg PA
CBHW020654220526
45464CB00001B/434